T0061912

AIDS Trauma and Support Group Therapy

Mutual Aid, Empowerment, Connection

MARTHA A. GABRIEL, PH.D.

THE FREE PRESS

New York   London   Toronto   Sydney   Singapore

THE FREE PRESS
A Division of Simon & Schuster Inc.
1230 Avenue of the Americas
New York, NY 10020

THE FREE PRESS and colophon are trademarks
of Simon & Schuster Inc.

Manufactured in the United States of America

10 9 8 7 6 5 4 3 2 1

Library of Congress Cataloging-in-Publication Data

Gabriel, Martha A.
    AIDS trauma and support group therapy: mutual aid, empowerment
connection / Martha A. Gabriel.
        p. cm.
    Includes bibliographical references and index.
    ISBN 978-1-416-57322-7
        1. AIDS (Disease)—Patients—Counseling of.   2. Group counseling.
I. Title.
RC607.A26G33   1996
616.97'92'0019—dc20   96–2932
                                                                    CIP

This book is dedicated to
those who have died from AIDS,
to those living with AIDS, and to those
who are working with persons with AIDS.

Contents

Acknowledgments

Through my work with volunteer mental health professionals who facilitated groups for persons with AIDS and for their carepartners and the staff at the Gay Men's Health Crisis, through my participation in a weekly support group, through my discussions and meetings with the staff of the AIDS program at Actors' Fund and social workers at St. Vincent's AIDS Center, through my experience as a facilitator of a weekly support group with New York University students in the School of Social Work, and through the narratives shared with me by people with AIDS, I have come to understand more deeply the dimensions of courage as well as the resiliency of the human spirit in struggling with matters of life and death. In all these instances, PWAs and professionals who abide with them shared generously their experiences, their observations, their despair, their hope, their outrage, and their awe. Their willingness to speak freely about themselves, this "illness," and the "work" made this book possible.

Of course, in every venture there are certain experiences that make an imprint. For me, being a group member of a weekly AIDS staff support group for some seven years was such an experience. Here I was able to fully appreciate the difficulty involved in attempting to articulate and tolerate the thoughts and feelings associated with AIDS work. It was here through observing, listening, talking, and being with a person with AIDS—my friend and colleague Lew Katoff—that I came to understand in a more vivid, often traumatic manner what it is like to bear witness to the dying of someone so alive. So I give special thanks to Lew and to my friends and colleagues in that group, especially Rande Turns and Andree Pilaro.

Although I am quite aware that the Gay Men's Health Crisis, Clinical Group Services as I knew it, introduced to me in 1986 by its innovative director, Richard Wein, has changed, I wish to recount the importance of that particular period in the history of both GMHC and AIDS services. The devotion and commitment of the volunteer therapists who facilitated weekly support groups, sometimes for as many as 1,200 PWAs per week, was one of the largest volunteer professional efforts in group therapy history. Their efforts and dedication to those they worked with is beyond measure. In appreciation of them and on their behalf, a portion of the revenues from this book will be donated to GMHC, Clinical Group Services. I especially thank Rande Turns, whose love of group services was reflected in his tenacious, vigilant protectiveness of our group services efforts. He was the heart and soul of group services.

Through writing this book, I became aware that social support is the remedy for most of us in confronting any and perhaps all life struggles. Leslie Rosenthal—group analyst/therapist, teacher, and sage—was essential to my efforts at writing this book and doing this work. Arnold Bernstein provided the perspective in his teachings that enabled me to learn how to "be" rather than focus "on becoming," and my analyst, Phyllis Meadow, provided an indescribable "life force." For technical and publishing support I was fortunate to benefit from the di-

Acknowledgments

rection, generosity, and graciousness of Free Press editor Susan Arellano, who made this task possible and enjoyable. I am also grateful to the late Shirley Ehrenkranz, Dean of the New York University School of Social Work, who was instrumental in providing me a Goddard Fellowship.

The major supports were my family and my family of friends: Mary Ann Jones, Barbara Nicholson, Jerry Matross, Barbara and Ben Dreyer, Hazel Weinberg, and Geri Truslow-Dawson. My sister-in-law Marie Ellen Monaco was particularly important to this venture, providing patient and loving computer consultation par excellence and conveying in all her instructions a sense of achievable mastery. Most of all, this effort would not have been realized without the consistent and loving support of Gail W. Monaco, who was in-house editor, consultant, companion, and, most of all, a loving spouse through all this. Thank you.

Introduction

This book was written to provide group practitioners and those interested in group practice with people with AIDS some understanding of the special considerations, difficulties, and challenges encountered in facilitating support groups for people traumatized by AIDS. The observations and illustrations provided are explored and discussed within the framework of trauma theory. AIDS-defined illness is thus understood as a traumatic stressor that may precipitate a host of traumatic stress reactions both in persons with AIDS (PWAs) and in those intensely involved with them. The role and value of support groups in managing such trauma is discussed. This book outlines group principles essential to the establishment of such groups and illustrates through narratives a host of different situations unique to support groups for people with life-threatening illnesses and particularly AIDS. The book may also serve as a reference for further readings, because each topic area is introduced through a review of the current AIDS-related literature in that area.

Chapter 1 provides the reader with a trauma framework wherein the development of an AIDS-defining opportunistic infection is conceptualized as a possible trauma with all the related psychological sequelae of trauma reactions. The reader is introduced to the theory of trauma, and a rationale is presented that links the reactions in some PWAs to those reactions described by other survivors of trauma. In the rest of the chapter, the theoretical underpinnings of support group therapy and its historical development is discussed. Special emphasis is given to the major elements in support group therapy: mutual aid, empowerment, and connection.

Chapter 2 provides a conceptual definition of support group therapy through discussion of four distinguishing characteristics: membership, dynamics of group, leadership, and group goals. Planning for a support group for people with AIDS is discussed by population, with special attention given to planning support groups for women with AIDS and for persons with AIDS who are chemically dependent. Since most current literature on PWAs reflects the experience of gay men in support groups, this literature is reviewed here. Specific issues in support group practice such as place, time, size, confidentiality, membership, and recruitment are presented and discussed.

Chapter 3 focuses on special issues and membership problems often encountered in such groups. Issues related to confidentiality in group practice are addressed, as well as special consideration/problems that may arise in these support groups. The impact of multiple deaths of group members is discussed with regard to the remaining members, the group as a whole, and the facilitators.

Chapter 4 focuses on the countertransference reactions in facilitators of support groups for PWAs, emphasizing the similarities to the countertransference reactions often experienced by other trauma therapists, i.e., those who work with Vietnam veterans, rape survivors, survivors of natural disaster, and survivors of massive violence. This chapter defines the term *countertransference* and reviews the role of countertransference in AIDS work. Its manifestations in groups and, in particular, AIDS support groups are elaborated upon through group illustrations and discussion.

In the concluding chapter, the effects of AIDS work on professionals working with PWAs are identified and discussed. The reader is introduced to the concepts of secondary traumatic stress, vicarious traumatization, and compassion fatigue. In this chapter Robert Lifton's conceptualization of survivor psychology is applied to the experiences of AIDS group facilitators. The course of secondary traumatic stress is examined as it unfolds around certain themes: the group facilitator's death imprint, psychic numbing, survivor's guilt, counterfeit nurturance, and search for meaning. These themes are illustrated through narratives provided by those who facilitate support groups for persons with AIDS.

CHAPTER 1

AIDS Trauma and Support Group Theory

Mutual Aid, Empowerment, and Connection

The reality of HIV/AIDS has over the course of the past decade and a half insinuated itself into everyday life and language. Though the "enemy," it is no stranger. It is in our social lives, our work, our homes, and our most intimate relationships. We know its curse; what remains elusive is its cure. When confronting an illness without a known cure, what becomes extremely important is the struggle to remain alive while maintaining hope of increasingly more effective treatments and, ultimately, a cure. For those who work with people with AIDS and listen to their narratives, who have witnessed their struggle and held out hope in the face of despair and trauma, the therapeutic value of mutual aid in the context of support groups, of the empowerment that comes from taking charge of one's health and illness is irrefutable. The tangible and intangible elements of social support and mutual aid as a force in dealing with the sequelae of trauma is the focus of this chapter.

AIDS AS A TRAUMATIC EVENT

PWAs are emerging as the newest group of persons experiencing psychological trauma. In describing elements of events that could be considered trauma-inducing, the trauma theorist Bonnie Green (1990) mentions seven: threat to one's life or bodily integrity, severe physical harm or injury, receipt of intentional injury/harm, exposure to the grotesque, violent/sudden loss of a loved one, witnessing or learning of violence toward a loved one, and learning of exposure to a noxious agent causing death or severe harm to another. AIDS survivors as well as AIDS health care professionals can quickly attest to the presence of some of these elements in varying degrees of intensity in their everyday lives. For those with AIDS, the initial diagnosis introduces a threat to their life, and the trajectory of the illness introduces enormous uncertainty and concerns with the possibility of physical deterioration. In addition, it is frequently the case that persons diagnosed with AIDS worry that they may have exposed others to the virus, thereby transmitting the disease. For the AIDS health care professional, the possibility of witnessing multiple deaths and struggles with the course of the disease looms large. Given the nature and dimensions of traumatic stress, it is reasonable to suggest that a diagnosis of AIDS constitutes a traumatic event. As McCann and Pearlman observed in their text (1990b) on the psychology of the adult trauma survivor:

Recent evidence suggests that this population is also at risk for PTSD (Martin, 1988). First, these individuals must face the prospect of premature death along with a serious decline in health, a difficult challenge common to all persons with serious illnesses. The diagnosis of any terminal illness disrupts one's schemas related to safety and invulnerability. The sense of un-certainty that accompanies exposure to the AIDS virus (e.g., will one utimately die or remain chronically ill with the AIDS Related Complex) is likely to be associated with feelings of personal vulnerability, fears about the future and a loss of hope about the future . . . Social isolation and the difficulty sustain-ing intimate connections may disrupt schemas for intimacy, re-sulting in feelings of alienation and estrangement from others. (pp. 305, 306)

The reactions and responses of PWAs to diagnosis and ill-ness fall well within the range of those experienced by trau-matized persons. Such reactions may be acute, prolonged, or chronic, depending on several factors. And in the case of PWAs, the stressor is chronic since it is continually life threat-ening. A further complicating factor is that not only are PWAs dealing with a threat to their own life but may be ac-tively witnessing the deterioration and death of their support network, i.e., "community trauma" (Shelby, 1995), thereby increasing their vulnerability to traumatic stress reactions (Keane, Scott, Chavoya, Lamparski, and Fairbanks, 1985). It important to distinguish between those with AIDS as a single stressor, prompting a traumatic stress reaction from those for whom AIDS is one of a host of traumatic stressors (i.e., domestic abuse, drug and alcoholic dependency, poverty, malnutrition, inadequate housing and access to medical treatments, random violence, and crime victimization). Although not specifically addressing the topic of life-threatening illness as an acute or chronic stressor, Baum, O'Keeffe, and Davidson (1990), writing on the topic of acute and chronic stress, articulate an important distinction:

> We have already considered that chronic stress lasts longer than acute stress, but we have been unable to specify what part or parts of the stress process are different. Stressor duration is potentially different, though for trauma most stressors are acute. Threat perception and appraisal may also vary. Acute threats are likely to be experienced as more intense than chronic threats . . . The threats posed by exposure to radiation during a nuclear accident, on the other hand, could pose clear, intense, acute threats and longer-term worries about the health effects to come. (p. 1647)

Utilizing this line of thinking, one might consider exposure to HIV similar to radiation exposure in that the long-term worries of the HIV-positive person may be considered chronic. These authors' designation of chronic traumatic events/stressors includes war, imprisonment, concentration camp, child abuse, spousal abuse, and toxic waste hazards. Although HIV/AIDS is not currently listed as a chronic traumatic event/stressor, it would appear to be one for many persons with HIV as well as those with an AIDS diagnosis. To some extent, it would appear to be so, for those health professionals who work intensely with them.

The Virus: HIV

The beginning of the HIV/AIDS pandemic in the United States was heralded by a small, almost unnoticed item appearing in the Centers for Disease Control *Morbidity and Mortality Weekly Review* (July 4, 1981), describing some common symptoms among a group of patients in both New York City and San Francisco. These conditions were Kaposi's sarcoma (KS), purplish lesions or patches appearing on the skin and affecting other organs like the lungs, heart, and, most often, the lymph nodes, and *Pneumocystis carinii* pneumonia (PCP). In the year following the first reports by the CDC, the center made reference to "homosexual or bi-sexual men" as the source of the illness, although clearly it would have been far more appropriate for the CDC to have spoken of particular behaviors as opposed to sexual orientation as its etiology. Its failure to do so had significant social, psychological, and cultural consequences, some of which are captured in the first name given to the AIDS virus: GRID—gay-related immune deficiency (Kain, 1989). GRID, generally thought of as the "gay plague," given its emphasis on gay life as the etiology of the disease, detoured early investigations from the study of the virus to examination of a lifestyle (Altman, 1986) and precipitated a nationwide epidemic of homophobia.

GRID, which later became known as AIDS (1984), acquired immune deficiency syndrome, is a term used to describe a host of infections that enter the body at "opportune" times, when the immune system is diminished, hence "opportunistic infections" (OIs). In addition to KS and PCP, other OIs were identified as associated with AIDS, e.g., toxoplasmosis, thrush, and cytomegalovirus. To the general term AIDS was added ARC (AIDS-Related Complex), a term that attempted to categorize the many debilitating symptoms such as fevers, sweats, persistent fatigue, diarrhea, and swollen glands that preceded the full-blown illness. Until 1993, such a wide range of symptoms required that the diagnosis of full-blown AIDS be predicated upon the appearance of particular "opportunistic infections." In 1993 the CDC expanded its definition of AIDS to include persons with a t-cell count (t-4 lymphocyte responsible for the proper functioning of the body's immune system) of below 200 and women with a host of other opportunistic infections, i.e., cervical cancer, pelvic inflammatory disease (PID), uterine tumors, and vaginal candidiasis, not ordinarily included in the CDC criteria of having AIDS (Denenberg, 1990).

Medical research in its quest for the answer to the question of etiology turned its attention away from the lifestyle hypothesis to a viral cause for AIDS in the late 1980s. Following on the heels of the discovery of the virus in 1988 (Gallo and Montagnier, 1988) came the development of a laboratory test to detect AIDS, enzyme-linked immunosorbent assay (ELISA). Such a test was primarily motivated by the demand to protect this country's blood supply from AIDS. Another more sensitive confirmatory test is the Western Blot. Both tests determine whether the person has been infected with HIV by indicating whether or not there are antibodies to the virus in the tested blood. With the use of ELISA and Western Blot, new terms emerged in the HIV/AIDS world: "seronegative," implying the absence of HIV antibodies, and "seropositive," implying the presence of HIV antibodies. The stress involved in being tested and its aftermath led to the formation of groups (both self-help and facilitated support groups) of "worried well" persons, either HIV positive or HIV negative, who came together to discuss their worries and anxieties about their health status. Concurrently drugs such as AZT (zidovudine), thought to be the first effective anti-AIDS agent, arrived on the market with great fanfare and engendered hope. Time and experience with AZT, however, highlighted its limitations and potentially disabling side effects (Rachlis, Peter, and Varga, 1993), especially for those without opportunistic infections. Currently a number of drugs are used to combat the progression of the virus or specific opportunistic infections, e.g., Bactrim, used for treatment of PCP, ddI (dideoxyinosine), foscarnet, peptide T, and a host of other drugs. Since 1987 major advances have been made in the understanding of the pathogenesis of the HIV virus and possible ways to inhibit its progression, including combining various drugs such as 3TC (lamivudine) in combination with AZT; ddC and d4T. Currently, work is in progress to develop a class of drugs called protease inhibitors (Gilden, 1995).[1] To date, however, AIDS continues to be an incurable transmittable disease. It is a stressor that constitutes a life-threatening situation of both an acute and chronic nature.

Surviving a Traumatic Stressor

Perhaps our most important source of knowledge regarding the psychological sequelae of diagnosis, illness, and multiple loss for PWAs is drawn from previous studies dealing with trauma survivors. Those studies (Danieli, 1985; Figley, 1987; Krystal, 1968; Lifton, 1979; Lindy, 1988; McCann and Pearlman, 1990; van der Kolb, 1984 and 1987; Wilson, Harel, Kahana, 1988) suggest that survivors of trauma exhibit a cluster of uniform responses that include distressing emotional reactions such as anxiety, dread, horror, fear, rage, shame, sadness, and depression; intrusive imagery of dying, nightmares, flashbacks of images of the stressor; numbing or avoidance of a situation associated with the images (included here is depersonalization, derealization, and dissociation); somatic complaints including sleep difficulties, headaches, gastrointestinal distress, and heart palpitations; behavioral response patterns including aggressive and antisocial behaviors, suicidal behaviors, substance abuse, and impaired social functioning; interpersonal difficulties; sexual dysfunction and difficulties sustaining intimate relationships.

People with AIDS often evidence a range of these reactions, often over the course of their illness. For some, the primary traumatic stressor is the diagnosis, for others the first opportunistic infection, for still others the first major physical impairment. In many instances the person with AIDS is traumatized from the day of diagnosis to the moment of death. The traumatization is further exacerbated by the simultaneous illness or loss of loved ones and the development of ever-increasing severe opportunistic infections. A common denominator of all psychological trauma according to Herman (1992) is a feeling of "intense fear, helplessness, loss of control and threat of annihilation" (p. 33). For the person with AIDS, the trauma may involve a prolonged psychological state including retraumatization with each new threat of OI and each loss of a friend or group member from AIDS.

More recent research (McFarlane, 1990; van der Kolk, 1987) on stressors and traumatic stress suggests that persons who develop traumatic stress reactions may have particular vulnerability to these reactions or disorders as a result of childhood traumas (Burnham, 1994; Cassese, 1993), an inadequate support system (Figley, 1986), recent stressful life changes, recent or chronic substance use (Keane, Gerardi, Lyons, and Wolfe, 1988), or the perception of the stressor as being outside their locus of control (Gerson and Carlier, 1992; Seligman, 1975).

Within this framework, the interventions that may be most helpful are those already identified as therapeutic with persons who have been traumatized. In the current literature on trauma and recovery from trauma, there is overwhelming endorsement of group intervention (Figley, 1986; Herman, 1992; Koller, Marmar, and Kanas, 1992; McCann and Pearlman, 1990b; van der Kolb, 1987).

Bessel M. van der Kolb (1987), a major traumatologist, discusses the role of group in trauma response, contrasting it to individual therapeutic intervention.

> It allows for more flexible roles, with mutual support and alternating positions of passivity and activity. In a group, patients can start re-experiencing themselves as being useful to other people. Ventilation and sharing of feeling and experiences in groups of people who have gone through similar experiences promotes the experience of being both victim and helper . . . In a group the therapists can facilitate re-empowerment by encouraging mutual support and by exploring the patient's resistance to taking an active role. (p. 163)

SUPPORT GROUPS

Historical Overview

Since its introduction in 1906 by Joseph Hershey Pratt, later named by Jacob L. Moreno in 1932, group therapy has undergone such a series of alternations resulting in a multiplicity of forms that in a recent comprehensive text on group psychotherapy (Yalom, 1995), it was suggested that it is best not to speak of group therapy as a single entity but as many distinct group therapies. While most of these group therapies subscribe in theory to the therapeutic factors identified by Yalom (1995)—instillation of hope, universality, imparting of information, altruism, corrective recapitulation of the primary family, development of socializing techniques, imitative behavior, interpersonal learning including insight, group cohesiveness, catharsis, and existential factors—each respective group therapy ascribes importance to and underscores specific elements as essential to its particular approach (Scheidlinger, 1993). For the type of group therapy conceptualized as support group therapy, the essential elements include instillation of hope, universality, imparting of information, altruism, group cohesiveness, catharsis, and existential factors. The concepts central to this particular form of group intervention are mutual aid, empowerment, and reconnection.

Consensus among historians (Anthony, 1971; Ettin, 1988; Mullan and Rosenbaum, 1978; Scheidlinger, 1993) appears to be that the method identified as support group therapy began formally in 1906. In that year, the first recorded group experience, known in current group literature as a support group, was described by Joseph Hershey Pratt in his article *The Home Sanatorium Treatment of Consumption* (cited in Ettin, 1988).

Pratt, a Boston internist, began working with tuberculosis patients in 1905. He observed what tuberculosis health providers continue to observe in tuberculosis patients, i.e., that persons with tuberculosis require rigorous follow-up to ensure that the treatments are effective. Pratt, in an effort to ensure effective treatments for patients, attempted to "indoctrinate" the patient to follow precise procedures for home care and hygiene. To accomplish this, he started "health classes" in a Boston church. As the weeks passed, he noted that the classes that involved significant or high degrees of group interactions exerted a positive influence on the patients' capacity to carry out home treatment plans. Pratt, apparently without conscious intention, had undertaken to treat the person in order to treat the disease through the development of a group class treatment. These class treatments included home visits and detailed record keeping, which included the patient's temperature, diet, and rest periods. All this material recorded by a group class member was reviewed by the physician and other group members. Testimonials and encouragements were given by successfully treated patients. Such testimonials appeared to be a primary means of expression and connection for the group members serving to combat the isolation and depression associated with tuberculosis.

These early "support groups" that involved a maximum of fifteen to twenty patients were homogeneous with regard to disease diagnosis and heterogeneous with regard to demographics and social status. Pregroup meetings involved group members acquainting the new members with the group rules, which, for the most part, addressed attendance and interaction. The actual process recorded by Pratt relied heavily on testimonials, much as the Alcoholics Anonymous groups would do later.

EMERGENCE OF SUPPORT GROUP THERAPY

Current interest in groups, particularly support groups, appears to have been fueled by two interrelated events. Just as group psychotherapy thrived during World War II, fueled by the need to provide psychiatric services to the returning veteran, so too did it burgeon during and following the Vietnam conflict. However, no longer was it spearheaded by the psychiatric or military establishment, as it had been in its beginning years, but rather by Vietnam veterans. In fact, for the veterans, it became a means to deal with the isolation and stigma they experienced on their return from the war. These early support groups basically consisted of veterans' "rap sessions" held in churches, community centers, and veterans halls throughout the United States. In such groups veterans shared with other veterans personal stories about their combat and postwar experiences. As a result of these rap sessions, most often facilitated by invited professional group leaders, the psychological community developed their knowledge base and deepened their understanding of reactions suffered and endured by these combat veterans (Keane, Caddell, and Taylor, 1988; Lindy, 1988; Solomon and Flum, 1988). Eventually such knowledge was more clearly conceptualized in psychological terms, through the formulation of the diagnostic category of posttraumatic stress syndrome entered the *American Psychiatric Association Diagnostic and Statistical Manual* in 1980 (Wilson, 1994). The recognition of the potentially distressing and sometimes debilitating consequences of combat trauma was a significant moment for veterans. Not only did it mean that literally thousands of veterans would qualify for a host of veteran-related health and mental health benefits but also that the isolation and stigma was finally recognized as contributing to a psychological condition. For group therapists, what emerged from these rap groups was a form of group therapy reminiscent of the original Pratt-type tuberculosis group.

In a similar mode, through consciousness-raising groups, rape crisis counseling groups, and groups for battered women, the women's movement began to examine some of the long-term consequences of violence toward women (Burgess and Holstrom, 1974; Steketee and Foa, 1989; Walker, 1991). In these groups, women sought to empower themselves, much in the same way the Vietnam veterans had achieved empowerment. As a result, shifts in social policy and human services began to emerge, resulting in an interest in and a focusing on the traumatic consequences of violence toward women (Herman, 1992). Taken collectively, the experiences of the combat veterans and the survivors of rape, battering, and child abuse have been quintessential to the development of a theory of support groups. This historical perspective suggests that support group therapy is a form of group intervention particularly suited for persons who have been traumatized by either natural or human-made catastrophic events. Support groups embrace the notion that their members have directly or indirectly been exposed to a traumatic stressor, i.e., to a situation wherein "a person has the personal experience of an event that involves actual or threatened death or serious injury or other threat to one's physical integrity; or witnessing an event that involves death, injury or a threat to the physical integrity of another person or learning about unexpected or violent death, serious harm or threat of death or injury experienced by a family member or other close associates." (American Psychiatric Association, 1994, p. 424).

THE CONCEPT OF MUTUAL AID
IN SUPPORT GROUP THEORY

Recent interest in the role of social support and mutual aid in health maintenance and disease etiology has increased in past decades, leading to a body of empirical data confirming that people with spouses, friends, and family members who provide psychological and material resources are in better health and deal more effectively with stress than those with fewer supportive social networks (Cobb, 1976; Cohen, 1988; Kaplan, Cassel, and Gore, 1979). In general the nature of social support is defined as the comfort, assistance, and/or information one receives through formal or informal contact with individuals or through groups. Flannery (1990), in the context of reviewing literature on social support and psychological trauma, identifies four types of social interactions that appear to mitigate the impact of a traumatic stressor: emotional support, information, social companionship, and instrumental support (providing tangible goods or favors). There have been three areas of inquiry related to social support and its role in recovery from trauma: trauma from combat, sexual assault, and battering. Flannery's review concluded that the cumulative research on this topic suggests an emerging understanding of the association between support and trauma recovery. A particularly significant study related to trauma from life-threatening illness—Spiegel, Bloom, Kraemer, and Gottheil (1989)—explored the effect of group intervention on time of survival of patients with metastatic breast cancer. In this study a ten-year follow-up revealed a significantly higher survival rate for the group that received the group intervention. Given certain parallels of the traumatic stress of cancer to that of HIV, this study can be viewed as providing more evidence for the group intervention in work with those with AIDS.

Social Support and HIV/AIDS

The belief that there are psychosocial factors, especially the presence and/or absence of social support, that have an effect on the immune system has been a growing area of investigation and remains an area open to continued inquiry (Perry, Jacobsberg, and Fishman, 1990; Stall, Coates, Mandel, Morales, and Sorensen, 1989). Empirical data reviewed by Kiecolt-Glaser and Glaser (1995) revealed an association between immunological alterations in cancer, infectious illness, HIV progression, and psycho stressors, particularly social supports. In an earlier work (1986), these authors examined specific data related to social supports and the immune system functioning of bereaved and divorced persons. Their findings suggested higher rates of both morbidity and mortality for both groups as a result of immune deregulation. Jemmott and Lock (1984) illustrated an association between life stress and immune systems deregulation through examination of epidemiological data of diseases such as acute respiratory infection, herpes simplex, mononucleosis, and tuberculosis. Taken collectively, these studies and reviews provide suggestive evidence of the association between social support and the immune system. While currently no firm conclusions have been reached, HIV/AIDS professionals need to be mindful of the potential and impact of support on the immune system.

Mutual Aid

These four social interactions defined by Flannery provide a framework for understanding the concept of mutual aid (Schwartz, 1974; Gitterman, 1989). It is the centrality of the concept of mutual aid that essentially distinguishes support groups from all other group therapies. Schwartz's observations on the concept of mutual aid emerged from his studies of small-group systems. Essentially Schwartz contends that all small groups have the following characteristics:

> First the group is an enterprise in mutual aid, an alliance of individuals who need each other, in varying degrees, to work on certain common problems. The important fact is that this is a helping system in which the clients need each other as well as the worker. The need to use each other, to create not one but many helping relationships, is a vital ingredient of the group process and constitutes a common need over and above the specific task for which the group was formed ... Second, the group itself, by the nature of its central problem, by the activities in which it engages, and by the particular personalities it brings together, creates its own conditions for success and failure ... Finally, the group is as we have indicated an organic whole: its nature cannot be discerned by analyzing the separate characteristics of each component but by viewing the group organism as a complex of moving, independent human beings, each acting out his changing relationships to society, in this present interaction with others engaged in a similar enterprise. (p. 218)

The concept of mutual aid developed from a parallel movement in the history of group psychotherapy that has its roots in the American Social Reform Movement of the 1920s and the American Settlement Movement. Modeled after the British Settlement Movement begun in England in 1884, the American Settlement House Movement emphasized small groups as a channel for social reform. Leaders such as Jane Addams, Florence Kelly, Lillian D. Wald, and others chose to settle and live in the poorest slums, introducing into their communities educational, cultural, and social reform opportunities. Such activities relied almost exclusively on mutual aid dynamics in which a small group of community residents was mobilized to address community stressors such as child care, aging, poverty, illiteracy, poor housing, child abuse, child labor protection, and women's rights. Through such collective action and mutual interest, the concept of mutual aid emerged. Such activities were especially appealing to new immigrant populations struggling with issues of acculturation, prejudice, and discrimination. Mutual aid became synonomous with settlement houses, which were established throughout the United States by the 1940s (Hull House, Chicago, founded by Jane Addams; South End House, started by Robert Woods in Boston, 1891; Henry Street Settlement, begun by Lillian Wald on the Lower Eastside of New York City; and the Chicago Common House, established by Graham Taylor in Chicago in 1894). These settlement houses organized neighborhoods into political forces that lobbied for and obtained advances in child labor law, public health, community child care services, and community-based adult educational services (Lee and Swenson, 1994). From it emerged a form of social work with groups that thrived in these settings. As the social worker theorists Germain and Gitterman (1980) observed, the model of group practice they represented by these settlement house activists was the "social goals model" of group work. It was conceptualized as

the development of personality to its greatest capacity; fostering of creative self-expression; the building of character and the improvement of interpersonal skills. For them group work functions also included the development of cultural and ethnic contributions; the teaching of democratic values; the support of active and mature participation in community life; the mobilizing of neighborhoods for social reform; and the preservation of ethical values. (p. 354)

Although this movement peaked in the era following World War II, current trends suggest a reemergence of the Settlement House Movement, stimulated by current legislative efforts to redesign health and welfare structures. For support group practice, the settlement houses provided illustration after illustration of the power of mutual aid and social supports.

THE CONCEPT OF EMPOWERMENT IN SUPPORT GROUPS

The AIDS epidemic has resulted in one of the most encompassing empowerment movements in past decades, the focus of which has been to empower persons diagnosed with a life-threatening illnesses to assume a more active "charge taking" stance with regard to their illness and treatment options. Such active as opposed to passively oriented responses are illustrated in the development of new terminology related to the nature of AIDS work, i.e., AIDS activist, AIDS advocacy, and AIDS initiatives, and by the formation of such organizations as the Gay Men's Health Crisis (GMHC), ACT-UP,[2] Shanti Project San Francisco, People with AIDS Coalition (PWA Coalition), Women at Risk (WAR), Body Positive, AIDS Treatment Data Network (ATDN), Community Health Project, and New York and Northern Lights Alternatives.

The term empowerment, derived from the Latin "potere," which means "to be able," has been used with increasing frequency in community psychology, social work, nursing, and other health and mental health literature. Viewed as a process of "becoming able" with the goal of "being able," empowerment carries a particular history and meaning for the oppressed. Both the process and the goal of empowerment involve attention to and adjustment of certain inequalities that impact on both access to power and distribution of power. Empowerment has been associated with such concepts as coping skills, mutual support, support system, community organization, neighborhood participation, personal efficacy, self-sufficiency, and self-esteem (Gibson, 1991).

For those confronting life-threatening illnesses, recent research (Flannery, Fulton, Tausch, and Deloffi, 1991; Flannery and Harvey, 1991) suggests that feelings of personal effectiveness and mastery (locus of control) are important to successful adaptation to certain stressful situations, particularly those associated with illnesses such as cancer and HIV/AIDS. The gay community, the first community massively affected by HIV/AIDS, has desperately struggled to embrace an active mode of response to the pandemic and in doing so has come to illustrate how empowerment strategies can be utilized.

Given the powerlessness associated with the trauma of a diagnosis of a life-threatening illness such as HIV/AIDS and the stigma associated with it, the concept of empowerment becomes central to any therapeutic or healing effort being orchestrated by PWAs. Essentially empowerment means "a process by which people, organizations or groups who are powerless (a) become aware of the power dynamics at work in their life context, (b) develop the skills and capacity for gaining some reasonable control over their lives, (c) exercise this control without infringing upon the rights of others, and (d) support the empowerment of others in their community" (McWhirter, 1991, p. 224).

Expanding and refining the parameters of the definition and meaning of empowerment for those diagnosed with HIV/AIDS is essential when considering certain populations, for example, the population of women currently struggling to live with the diagnosis of HIV/AIDS. Theorists writing on women's development, Jean Baker Miller and Irene Stiver (1993), view empowerment through the larger lens of power through connection. These writings and others suggest that women's sense of development with regard to coping skills and control over their lives is essentially related to the establishment of mutually empathetic and empowering relationships with others (Jordan, Kaplan, Miller, Stiver, and Surrey, 1991). In considering and conceptualizing the plight of women diagnosed with HIV/AIDS, it is important to consider not only the universal but also the particulars of a given situation to understand and tap into the full meaning and method of empowerment for them.

With the advent of empowerment movements came the emphasis on survivor rather than victim. The language of "surviving" shifts the conceptualization of victimization from victim to survivor, from hopeless to hopeful, from powerless to empowering. This language has been used to underscore the distinct features of survival: it is ongoing and the traumatic effect is temporarily, if not permanently weathered, and although something life-threatening has occurred or may be occurring, life has been sustained (Rappaport, 1985).

The reality of empowerment for the PWA entails little if any separation between the personal and the political. As Gutierrez (1990) observed, empowerment is "a process of increasing personal, interpersonal, or political power so that individuals can take actions to improve their life situations (p.

193). She further suggested four identifiable psychological changes associated with the empowerment process: The first is self-efficacy, defined as the belief in one's ability to produce and reevaluate events in one's life. This process involves what is described in the clinical literature as ego strengthening, a sense of personal power and mastery and an increased ability to act on one's behalf. Second, the process entails the development of group consciousness, created within the individual or among members of a group or community that has a sense of a shared fate. Third, the process involves a reduction in self-blame achieved through attributing some of the current disempowerment to forces outside the self, i.e., in society or to fate. Finally, the assumption of personal responsibility for change occurs as a goal of this process.

Illustrations of empowerment efforts by PWAs are manifested in the changes that have occurred in biomedical research, in the delivery health care services, and in changes in protocols for drug treatment interventions. In addition, PWAs have participated on advisory boards drafting federal, state, and municipal guidelines for addressing the financing, service delivery, and ethical issues that continue to emerge.

Gutierrez as well as other theorists (Pinderhughes, 1983; Rappaport, 1985; Gibson, 1991; McWhirter, 1991) writing on empowerment suggests that the small-group method is the ideal with regard to empowerment interventions. Gutierrez states:

> group work is presented as the ideal modality for empowering interventions, because it is an effective means for integrating the other techniques . . . The groups facilitate empowerment by creating a basis for social support through the change

process, a format for providing concrete assistance, an opportunity to learn new skills through role playing and observing others and a potential power base for future actions. (p. 195)

THE CONCEPT OF CONNECTION IN SUPPORT GROUPS

The concept of connection was explicated by John Bowlby (1969, 1973) in his work on attachment theory. In his two-volume work, Bowlby conceptualized the various internal processes and behaviors associated with the concept of attachment. Essentially, attachment refers to those dynamics which create the emotional bonds connecting the individual to family, friends, and community. While attachment creates connections, trauma shatters them. Trauma theorists have repeatedly called attention to the emotional disconnection prompted by traumatic events. Lindemann (1944), writing on his observations of the effects of trauma, essentially defined trauma as "the sudden uncontrolled severance of affective ties" (p. 40). Krystal (1968), writing several decades later on the topic of the massive trauma that arose out of the Holocaust, spoke of disrupted "human connection" that results from acute traumatic states. The individual in such a disrupted state "stands alone and abandoned by all sources of feelings of security" (p. 14). More recently Herman (1992) observed that "traumatic events have primary effects not only on the psychological structure of the self but also on the systems of attachment and meaning that link individual and community" (p. 51). A full conceptualization of the impact of trauma on the attachment life of individuals emerges in the work of Ronnie Janoff-Bulman (1985, 1992). In her conceptualization, disconnection is manifested in three realms of assumptions that organize cognitive life. These assumptions include a belief in personal invulnerability, a perception of the world as meaningful, and a perception of ourselves as positive and capable. These beliefs in Janoff-Bulman's view constitute the assumptive world that trauma ultimately shatters. Such shattering leaves individuals disconnected from the belief system that previously governed their life pursuits. And such shattering produces a sense of profound vulnerability. Emotional management and eventual mastery within this context may lead to a self-identity of survivorship. The person with AIDS on learning of an AIDS-defining diagnosis, on daily confronting the uncertainties and challenges of living with AIDS, is often caught in an emotional maelstrom that runs the gamut from acute to subacute to chronic trauma. With the diagnosis comes the sense of personal vulnerability and the fear that one's body has failed. The belief in a world as meaningful may be suddenly shattered by the realization that one's life may be shortened and one's life plan interrupted. Quest for meaning may be manifested in the forms of such questions as why did this happen to me. The sense of self as positive and powerful often yields, hopefully temporarily, to feelings of powerlessness and helplessness in the face of a disease that has many variations and the potential to progress aggressively despite vigorous treatment efforts. The shattering of assumptions and the consequent disconnection from one's sense of self and sense of the world is the raw material out of which the sense of survivorship may emerge. For the group practitioners working with PWAs, this transformation, movement from disconnection to reconnection and reconstruction, is the heart of the emotional work done in these support groups.

Given the quintessential role of connection in the healing

of trauma, the concept of connection as it has emerged in the literature on female development (Gilligan, 1982; Belenky, Clinchy, Goldberger, and Tarule, 1986; Jordan, Kaplan, Miller, Stiver, and Surrey, 1991; Miller and Stiver, 1993) warrants considerably more attention, especially in light of the current predications that ever-increasing numbers will be diagnosed and traumatized by AIDS, particularly women of color (Mays and Cochran, 1988; Nichols, 1989). Jordan, Kaplan, Miller, Stiver and Surrey's (1991) work in developmental psychology illustrates the centrality of the sense of connection in women's lives. These observations provide a framework for understanding how trauma might be perceived as ultimately destroying the sense of self derived from being in a relationship. This recognition of relationship as the source of power and effectiveness for women needs to be an essential element in the development of any therapeutic or healing efforts directed toward women.[3] According to Herman (1992), what impels people to withdraw during periods of trauma while desperately wishing for relatedness is the profound disruption in basic trust and the common feelings of shame. This withdrawal may be heightened in the case of AIDS by the associated stigma, guilt, and shame that is too frequently associated with this diagnosis. The withdrawal serves to help the survivor, in this case the PWA, avoid any reminders of the diagnosis or the illness. Such withdrawal may be from family, friends, previous lovers, even from visiting familiar places or going to familiar events. And as expected, the more isolated PWAs are, the more terrorized they become; this leads to a heightened state of disconnection, the very outcome the PWA fears the most. Such isolation deprives PWAs of the comfort that contact under these circumstances would normally provide. As one young woman reflected, reporting on her first reaction to the diagnosis of AIDS, which was given during a prenatal clinic visit:

> No way you would know what was going on in my mind. I have never before been so terrified or felt so helpless. I felt the whole world had kicked everything out from under me. I was alive but adrift in darkness. I had nightmare after nightmare. Being with my family and them knowing made me feel even more outside of it all. Being with them or anyone else meant nothing to me. I thought how will my kids survive without me. I felt so utterly alone. I know I will tell them. But then they will have to deal with all this shit coming my way. Will they be teased and isolated at school? Will they go on and be able to learn, knowing all this? How will they manage?

Central to the movement from disconnection to reconnection and reconstruction is the activity of narration, or storytelling. A completed narrative "gives sense to" or "makes sense of" a particular set of experiences. This meaning-making activity is crucial to restoring connection to others. Wigren (1994), writing on narrative completion in the treatment of persons who have been traumatized, observed:

> Trauma disrupts the social connections that facilitate storymaking. This can occur in a number of different ways. Trauma victims may feel alienated from others simply by virtue of the difference between their own overwhelming preoccupation with the trauma and others' involvement in the mundane events of everyday life. Further because trauma is painful for audiences as well as victims others may withdraw from the victim in order to avoid or defend against this pain. This is true on both societal

and personal levels. When others withdraw, the reality of traumatic experience is disconfirmed, and the social world of the victim constructs a story that does not include the story of his or her experience. Finally trauma victims are actively silenced. (p. 417)

Narrative development appears central to psychological organization as well as serving as the connection between self and others. Narratives according to Wigren organize and contain affect while the creation of a narrative provides a cognitive context for felt experience, thereby making the narrative the link between mind and body.

The facilitating of storymaking and storytelling that becomes central to coping with and recovery from the traumatic consequence of AIDS is synonymous with the creation of meaning and is the core element in support groups. For the person with AIDS confronted by experiences of stigma and discrimination, connection to others through storytelling is essential. It is a means of communicating that, through time and repetition, holds the possibility of leading to feelings of connection, support, and empowerment. In a recent article on narrative as an approach to understanding a gay man's AIDS support group, Dean (1995) observes:

Narratives have had many meanings and uses in the group. They allow members to dilute and counteract negative ideas and images in their lives and in the dominant culture. They are also used to confirm and celebrate gay culture. They permit the maintenance of integrity and identity. They provide opportunities for joining and enlarging each other's experiences and creating community. They also bring about mourning and coming to terms with limitations in an atmosphere of comfort and acceptance. The telling and sharing of stories become acts of creation in the face of death. (p. 298)

Connection to Community

Studies of survivor groups (Danieli, 1985; Lindy, 1988; Herman, 1992) have suggested that the response of the larger community, outside the kinship group, is also a source of an important connection for those surviving a traumatic experience. When there is a breach between survivor and community, the recovery from such a breach appears to rest on two important factors: public acknowledgment of the traumatic event and some form of community action both to assign responsibility for the harm and to repair the injury (Herman, 1992). Such community response in the face of a traumatic circumstance assists in reconnecting the survivor. A historical and no less shameful example of the response of many communities to PWAs is the community rejection involved in this nation's responses to returning Vietnam veterans who, upon arrival home, were met with stigma, rejection, detachment, and often direct expressions of hostility from the public on whose behalf they had risked their lives. It was only with the construction of the Vietnam War Memorial in Washington, D.C., in 1987 that community acknowledgment of the "sorrow" and grief experienced by these soldiers began.

In the first decade of the HIV/AIDS epidemic, the AIDS activist movement has, by and large, succeeded in providing a forum in which these two above-mentioned conditions of a connective response from the community were met. Through the ACT-UP organization, with its chapters throughout the United States and in parts of Europe, and activism by other

AIDS organizations and grassroots groups, the public at large became more aware of and often involved in the battle against the virus. A significant expression of public awareness and action toward healing and bridging the disconnection experienced by PWAs, their families, lovers, and friends has been through the "Quilt Project," which captures the names and stories of many of those who have died from AIDS.[4]

SUMMARY

Using a current understanding of trauma and trauma reactions, this chapter focused on elements essentially for recovery from the trauma precipitated by the diagnosis of an AIDS-defined infection. It outlined the importance of understanding the sequelae of reactions reported by other survivors of trauma events and identified three essential elements: the importance of mutual aid, the enhancement of self-esteem through active behaviors that provide a sense of empowerment, and the need for connection with others, particularly those who have been traumatized by the same if not similar stressor. These elements are essential to support group therapy and are identified as the central healing forces in support groups for people with AIDS.

CHAPTER 2

Definition, Planning, Populations, and Structure for Support Groups with PWAs

It would seem plausible to suggest that most persons with AIDS suffer traumatic response at some point in the trajectory of this disease and thus react in much the same way as other survivors of trauma (Figley, 1987; Green, Wilson, and Lindy, 1985; Herman, 1992; McCann and Pearlman, 1990b). Given this, perhaps our best efforts at effectively ameliorating the psychological sequelae of AIDS trauma need to be organized around the observations of trauma theorists over the past three decades. The clinical experience of trauma theorists, also called traumatologists (Figley, 1987; van der Kolk, 1984; McCann and Pearlman, 1990b; Janoff-Bulman, 1985; Herman, 1992), have led each to regard group intervention as the most effective form of intervention with trauma survivors, including persons with AIDS (McCann and Pearlman, 1990b;

Green, 1990; Janoff-Bulman, 1985). Although a paucity of literature exists on group treatment with PWAs, those authors (Beckett and Rutan, 1990; Buck, 1991; Daniolos, 1994; El-Mallakh and El-Mallakh, 1989; Field and Shore, 1992; Gabriel, 1991; Getzel, 1994; Getzel and Mahony, 1990; Kelly and Sykes, 1989; Newmark, 1984; Nichols, 1984; Norsworthy and Horne, 1994; Ribble, 1989; Sageman, 1989; Spector and Conklin, 1987; Tunnell, 1991, 1994) who do write on the subject overwhelmingly identify a support group model that relies on the processes of mutual aid, empowerment, and reconnection as the model of choice.

Though a precise definition of support group therapy is lacking in current group literature, it is most often identified by its central features (Rosenberg, 1984; Yalom, 1995). Though seldom conceptualized simultaneously, these include the basic elements of mutual aid, empowerment, and reconnection. Given this conceptual framework, support group therapy may be defined as a group intervention whereby those with similar traumatic stress situations and stressors come together under the auspices of a trained group facilitator(s) for the purpose of healing the psychic injury induced by trauma through mutual aid, empowerment, and reconnection. The term *healing* is used here to emphasize that traumatic stress reactions are not viewed as pathological in most instances and thereby do not require the traditional curative intervention model.

DEFINITION: FOUR CHARACTERISTICS OF SUPPORT GROUPS

Support groups are characterized by specific features in terms of membership, group dynamics, leadership, and group goals. In contrast to other therapies that seek heterogeneity, in support group therapy there is homogeneity with regard to the nature of the traumatic stressor. Sameness is sought in one singular area, that of the stressor or stress situation. This factor of commonality of stressors accelerates the development of group cohesiveness, which is often described in group literature as the "attractiveness of the group for its members" (Yalom, 1995). For example, note the homogeneity of the traumatic stressors in support groups for survivors of rape, incest, domestic violence, cancer, or HIV/AIDS.

Essentially, the members present their trauma, not themselves, as the problem. Stressors can be transitory, i.e., persons just released from the hospital after major surgery (e.g., heart bypass surgery, breast surgery), persons who were in major accidents, or persons who witnessed violence. Other stressors are more crisis-oriented, e.g., the aftermath of a natural disaster or terrorism. There can be chronic stressors, such as a chronic physical illness or a chronic mental disorder. In each situation the members are viewed as survivors of traumatic stress events. Viewing members as survivors becomes important in understanding the differences between support group therapy and other group therapies, both in terms of the nature of the group and the role of the facilitator.

Membership: Screening

The pregroup screening process in AIDS support groups is more abbreviated than most other pregroup screening efforts. In most of the literature on pregroup screening (Couch, 1995; Frances and Dugo, 1985; Jones and Crandall, 1985;

Yalom, 1995), emphasis is placed on careful and, frequently, lengthy pregroup screening and preparation. Sometimes the pregroup screening and preparation process involves written as well as verbal exchange, along with several individual sessions with the group therapists prior to initiation into a group (Yalom, 1995). Since support groups do not focus on achieving a level of heterogeneity of members, nor are they concerned with presenting problems or character change, the screening interviews can often be done in small groups of two or three prospective members. In screening interviews for AIDS support groups, the facilitators are concerned with stage of illness of the member, type of opportunistic infections, amount of physical distress the PWA is experiencing, level of financial and emotional support available to the PWA, and probability of psychiatric or neurological impairments related to the AIDS diagnosis. In talking with the PWA about the support group, the facilitators are interested in assessing how the person has been coping with the trauma of HIV/AIDS and whether the PWA has the willingness and/or the capacity to talk with others about his or her reactions. What qualifies a person for group membership is the "universality of the experience." The facilitator's focus in the interview is the prospective members' willingness to construct an AIDS narrative. Despite differences in age, race, gender, socioeconomic status, ethnicity, and sexual orientation, the common traumatic stressor provides a shared language, in this instance the AIDS language, e.g., t-cells, viral load, nonprogressors, antivirals, AZT, protease inhibitors, MAI, and so on. It is important, however, to emphasize that a group member may derive enormous help from a support group even without uttering a word (Yalom, 1995; Herman,

1992), since the power of listening to the trauma narratives of others can be healing in and of itself.

Dynamics of Support Group Therapy

Rosenberg (1984) observed, "the support group is used for reinforcement rather than for reconstruction" (p. 177). Such a statement reveals the crucial difference between support group therapy and other group therapies. For support group participants, it is the positive reinforcement of effective coping behaviors and the interpersonal insights related to improving coping patterns that fuel the interchanges between and among members. The focus of control for the group's work lay with its members, who tell their trauma stories, give advice, make suggestions, test reality, empathize, and ultimately support each others' effort. The emphasis is on safety, mutual aid, and empowerment instead of identification of problem, behavioral modification, or personality change.

Leadership: Facilitation

Leaders of support groups are thought of as facilitators. As such, the healing derived from the support group experience relies not so much on the skills of the leader in terms of recon-structive or interpretive abilities but primarily on the capacity of the group with the facilitators' framing to provide a safe en-vironment conducive to the emergence of mutual aid behav-iors necessary for healing and coping. Several features distin-guish group facilitation in support groups from traditional group leadership. One such distinguishing feature is the trans-parency of the leader's role in the group. Yalom (1995) speaks of the necessary transparency in the group psychotherapy process; in support groups, this transparency is not only necessary but often more tangible. For example, in an AIDS support group, the facilitator may or may not be affected by the same traumatic stressor (a diagnosis of HIV positive or an opportunistic infection) as the group members, and may ultimately disclose this information and other information in the service of the progressive functioning of the group. A second distinguishing feature pertains to the fact that emphasis in support group therapy is on the "bridging function" (Ormont, 1990), i.e., the facilitators of a support group work as a conduit providing a lineage between members, especially in the initial stages of the support group meetings.[1] In connecting through "bridging," the facilitator assists the members in talking about similarities and/or differences not only in terms of the course of AIDS and as a physical entity but also in terms of how the illness has affected their lifestyles and characters. Thus task facilitation is guided by weaving connections among members, with the goal of achieving a deep sense of cohesiveness. Facilitators of support groups need to take the primary initiative in building bridges between and among members to provide a "sense of community," which Herman (1992) suggests is essential to the therapeutic process of support groups.

Support group facilitators tend to focus on the role of helping the group become the prototype of a well-regulated family or kinship group, providing its members with a safe emotional environment and thus affording them an opportunity to talk not only about their respective responses to stressors but to identify with various coping styles. Commenting on the healing capacity of support groups for the traumatized Herman (1992) observed:

Traumatic events destroy the sustaining bonds between individual and community. Those who have survived learn that their sense of self, of worth, of humanity, depends upon a feeling of connection to others. The solidarity of a group provides the strongest protection against terror and despair, and the strongest antidote to traumatic experience. Trauma isolates; the group re-creates a sense of belonging. Trauma shames and stigmatizes; the group bears witness and affirms. (p. 214)

Goals in Support Group Therapy

As already mentioned, the goal in support group therapy is the enhancement of coping skills through mutual aid, empowerment, and reconnection. Since members in these groups are typically confronting some extraordinary traumatic stressor, they often turn urgently to one another, telling their own stories of trauma while listening to the stories of other members. An illustration of the mutual aid principle and its potential for enhancing coping skills occurred in a support group for care partners of PWAs. A prospective group member attending her first meeting after numerous cancellations started telling her AIDS narrative:

> I have come tonight, because I finally think I can talk about my "situation." I survived many things, drug abuse, getting beaten by my husband, but I don't know if I can survive telling my kids the real story about me and their father. Can any of you help me figure out how I am going to tell my kids that their father is dying . . . that I may die and that they may be orphans? One is 15 and one is 16 and they depend on me a lot . . . for everything.

Member A: My kids don't know about my situation. I'm still OK. They wouldn't be able to handle the information. I say, why say anything right now, what's the hurry?

Member B: If you want to know I can tell you what I did in telling my son about my condition. It was tough but he's handling it and it is much better between us. In fact when I told him, he was relieved because now he could talk to me about what he already thought was happening.

Member C: Kids are smart. They may already know. But I think you need some help in telling them. I mean, you're not just telling them about you but about their father.

Such examples are numerous and illustrate the process of mutual aid, empowerment, and connection within the support group context.

PLANNING A SUPPORT GROUP FOR PEOPLE WITH AIDS

As a traumatized population, PWAs present group facilitators with a particular therapeutic challenge because HIV illness adds a particular complexity to the group processes. More specifically, group members are dealing with the threat of a drastically shortened life span with few curative treatment options; they are witnessing the deterioration and deaths of group members, as well as the deaths and deterioration of others in support networks; they are confronting an illness with an unpredictable course that has a powerful societal stigma (Gabriel, 1991; Herek and Glunt, 1988; Tunnell, 1991). Although HIV/AIDS presents complexities similar to those discussed in group psychotherapy with persons with cancer (Daste, 1990; Ferlic, Goldman, and Kennedy, 1979;

Ringler, Whitman, Gustafson, and Colemn, 1981; Spiegel and Glafkides, 1983; Spiegel, Bloom, and Yalom, 1981), it differs in several important aspects. Cancer presents an array of treatment options with the potential for complete remission, it affects the general population more proportionately, and it is not associated with contagion and is not identified as stigmatizing. AIDS, on the other hand, currently has no cure, affects populations where stressors tend to be the greatest, is contagious, and ultimately is stigmatizing.

An alarming feature is that those currently the most affected by AIDS are young women living in poverty who are already disempowered and confronting a multiple of stressors such as malnutrition, single parenting, and inadequate housing and medical care. In addition, many are survivors of previous trauma such as child abuse (Burnham, 1994), domestic violence (Herman, 1992), rape, and random violence (McCann and Pearlman, 1990b).

Given the multiple stressors associated with having AIDS, particularly the stigma associated with it, such routine matters as announcing a group, locating potential members, screening members, planning group, size, deciding time and place offer administrative and therapeutic challenges to agencies, medical centers, and group facilitators. Recruitment has generally involved careful consideration of all the associated factors, particularly issues of stigma and the need for confidentiality. In addition, it is important for facilitators to understand in some more elaborate way the host of psychosocial stressors confronting the person with AIDS. Knowledge of such stressors confronting potential group members is essential to the planning process. Facilitators must possess sufficient knowledge of HIV/AIDS and its relationships with other stressors, because for the majority of persons with HIV/AIDS, the virus is bu one of a series of stressful events.

Planning a Support Group for Women with AIDS

Who are these women with AIDS? Demographically, the) tend to be intravenous drug users or they have had unprotected sex with men who have used IV drugs; women whc carry a dual diagnosis of a mental illness and chemical dependency; lesbians who have high-risk sex with both women and men who have HIV/AIDS; women in correctional institutions, who currently are living half as long as their HIV/AIDS male counterparts (Brettle and Lean, 1991; Christensen, 1992; Denenberg, 1994).

Although women will constitute the largest proportion of new HIV/AIDS cases by the end of this decade, they have been essentially underdiagnosed, and undertreated, underreported, and are ultimately invisible (Cochran and Mays, 1989; Chu, Buehler, and Berkelman, 1990; Denenberg, 1990, 1994; Hunter, 1995). Comparatively little is known about the course and treatment of HIV/AIDS in women.[2] In contrast to the virus in men, which focused initially on KS and PCP, HIV in women involves organ-specific infections that include such diseases as pelvic inflammatory disease (PID), endometriosis, uterine tumors, cervical cancer, vaginal candidiasis, higher incidences of some conditions (like simple urinary tract infections, human papillomavirus infection [HPV]), and increased complications associated with infection such as gonorrhea and chlamydia (Denenberg, 1994).

Structural problems endemic to health care and the welfare structure of this country create formidable barriers to physical and mental health for poor and working-class women who have HIV/AIDS.

Martha Ward (1993), a social anthropologist, conceptualizes the experience and impact of HIV/AIDS as a different disease for women and particularly for poor women:

> HIV/AIDS for poor women is not a new disease; it is only another life-threatening condition which parallels serious health problems already experienced by these populations. A time-honored and broad continuum of disease and death for poor women is linked to such factors as poverty, self-medication, infant morbidity, infant mortality and cervical cancer. The programmatic responses to HIV/AIDS in poor women have been grafted onto existing services established by and for homosexual men or onto the obstetrical-gynecological and prenatal systems already in place. . . . These conclusions lead to somber predictions for the course of the epidemic and the prognosis for treatment and care for poor women with HIV. (p. 413)

The group facilitator planning to recruit women with HIV/AIDS needs to be aware that women, for the most part, organize their activities around caring, generally care-taking functions, i.e., generally for or coordinating care of their own children or children of significant others. Therefore, maternal and child health care services are often the place where they may first obtain HIV services and thus where support groups may find their membership. However, women who come to such services, whether they be large hospital centers or smaller, community-based health care centers, are often preoccupied with the complicated, time-consuming, difficult processes of registering and obtaining clinic care with their sick child or children in tow, not to mention their anxiety about eligibility for services. For working women with children, there are transportation problems, child care problems, inconvenient clinic hours, and long waits both for appointments and again in the clinics. Language barriers, insensitive communication styles, and cultural incompatibilities between the clinical providers and the women with HIV/AIDS reinforce an already deteriorated health delivery system. All these factors make the recruitment of women difficult and may be one of the myriad reasons why support groups with women who have HIV/AIDS is a neglected area of attention or interest in the group literature. To achieve successful recruitment of women, group practitioners must be prepared to find creative, nontraditional ways to engage potential women members in forming a support group.

Support Groups for Women with AIDS and Chemical Dependency

In general, chemically dependent women are poorer, less educated, and less skilled, and have less paid work experience than chemical-dependent men. Much of their energy is consumed with basic survival, especially if they are caring for small children. Recent research suggests that chemically dependent women have greater incidence of extensive sexual and physical abuse (Boyd, 1993; Kane-Cavaiola and Rullo-Cooney, 1991). In fact, Boyd's study reported that 61 percent of chemically dependent women have been sexually abused, 67 percent of them prior to the age of seventeen. Women are reported to be more socially isolated and detached from peers, particularly those who are single parents, than men. In addition, there appears to be greater social stigma attached to substance abuse in women than in men, and women are more likely to be rejected by family and friends than are chemically dependent men. Since women are primary caregivers and often provide for dependent children, chemically addicted women in treatment facilities frequently refer to child care and parenting responsibilities as central to their lives, as well as a significant barrier to getting and sustaining treatment for their addiction problem. Studies of women seeking substance abuse treatment often cite lack of child care as a primary obstacle to program attendance (Zankowski, 1987). Reproductive status also provides an obstacle to women seeking treatment, since few addiction treatment programs admit pregnant women. Women with chemical dependency are for the most part isolated, stigmatized, and disconnected from a natural network of supports, as well as from traditional treatment services. This is a tragic state of affairs, without factoring in the consequences of an HIV/AIDS diagnosis and illness, which, of course, further exacerbates all of the above-mentioned factors and further diminishes treatment options. Of the options discussed in the current literature for chemically dependent women, the most successful are groups for "women only." Kauffman, Dore, and Nelson-Zlupko's 1995 article on the role of women's therapy groups in the treatment of chemically dependent women observed the therapeutic power of the women-only support group. They stated:

> Women-only groups allow chemically dependent women to find other women potential sources of support and nurturance as well as models of power and independent action. Many addicted women have experienced maternal rejection and abandonment as children. Many have also observed the powerlessness of their mothers to protect themselves and their children

from sexually abusive, violent husbands and fathers, thus internalizing a view of women as passive victims. According to the respondents, women's groups afforded them opportunities to experience other women as responsive and caring, as well as to observe and understand the effects of victimization on others, and this empowered them in their quest for sobriety and personal change. (p. 361)

Persons with HIV/AIDS and Chemical Dependency

In the early years of this epidemic it was apparent that the sharing of drug injection paraphernalia, especially needles among heroin-addicted persons, was a critical element in HIV transmission (Caputo, 1985). The prevalence of crack use in the 1980s deepened social problems in the inner cities, which were already affected by HIV/AIDS. Crack increased the likelihood of high-risk sexual behaviors among users of all ages, particularly adolescents. This coupled with intravenous heroin use constituted a major risk factor for the spread of HIV illness (Tierney, 1990).[3] In addition, there was a rise in the number of babies born who showed evidence of maternal cocaine use. The "crack babies" burdened the mother with AIDS even more as she confronted her illness, as well as the potential for HIV in her infant. Such infants, as is well documented (Levine, 1993), need intensive medical care following birth and often even more care if the possibility of having HIV is realized. Because of legal sanctions against the possession of drugs and injection equipment, many users seem inclined to "shoot up" shortly after a drug purchase in "shooting galleries" that flourished as "communal injection" sites. So much attention has been focused on IV drug use behavior that little is known about the addicted person. Often case illustrations in journals and texts described the drug use pattern but give little information about the drug user's life and struggles. For this reason and perhaps because of gender and racial bias, little if anything is known about the specifics of the chemically dependent person's life, with or without HIV. For the group facilitator this population is perhaps the most difficult to engage. Not only are its members more frequently the survivors of multiple trauma but they also are more profoundly isolated by an AIDS diagnosis, given society's view of drug dependence and by the legal sanctions against these behaviors (Honey, 1988).

Gay Men with HIV/AIDS

Of all those persons diagnosed with HIV/AIDS, we have learned the most about and from studies of gay men with regard to diagnosis, course of illness, and treatment and survival. Since gay men (Cadwell, 1994b) were the first identified group, a model of both medical and psychosocial treatment evolved based on their experiences and outcomes of treatment. Only recently has it become clear that models for treatment of white, middle-class, homosexual men are not necessarily applicable to other populations of PWAs. Literature on support groups for HIV/AIDS has relied heavily on the experiences of facilitators in groups for gay men with HIV/AIDS. In fact, a large part of our understanding of support group processes is derived observation and the study of gay men with HIV/AIDS in support groups (Beckett and Rutan, 1990; Gambe and Getzel, 1989; Field and Shore, 1992; Getzel and Mahony, 1990; Norsworthy and Horne, 1994; Tunnell, 1991, 1994).

In the majority of situations, gay men have proven to be eager, articulate, and highly motivated toward group participation. Group services such as those provided by the Gay Men's Health Crisis during the period 1986–92 worked with, on average, a total of one thousand gay men per month in weekly hour-and-a-half support group meetings facilitated by volunteer group practitioners. By and large these group were dominated by the presence of gay men who carried a diagnosis of AIDS and were struggling with various issues related to their illness, i.e., revealing diagnosis, medication and other treatment decision, issues related to relationships and sexuality, and fears related to the course of illness and death. A by-product of these groups was a knowledge of the importance of homogeneity among group members with regard to diagnosis (Gabriel, 1991). Several issues appear central to the struggle of gay men with AIDS, issues that have been addressed by various practitioners reflecting on the experience of gay men (Martin, 1991; Tunnell, 1994). First, in addition to feeling the stigma of having been diagnosed, the gay PWA also bears the stigma of being homosexual. Much has been written about which stigma is more devastating to gay men—having AIDS or being homosexual (Cadwell, 1994; Herek and Glunt, 1988; Shilts, 1987). Second, in acknowledging an AIDS diagnosis, many gay men are painfully confronted with "unfinished business" related to their own acceptance of their homosexuality (Martin, 1991). Third, perhaps the consequence of homophobia, is the dynamic of counterdependence often circumscribing the relationships of gay men wherein the wish to be dependent and intimate with other men is carefully defended against (Tunnell, 1994).

Thus it is essential for facilitators to be familiar with and attuned to the special issues related to homosexuality in facilitating AIDS support groups with gay men. Unacknowledged internalized homophobia within facilitators and within group members has enormous power to undermine the group's ability to achieve real connection and healing.

Planning for Support Groups in Rural Communities

Traditionally members for a group are obtained through a variety of means, i.e., referral from health or mental professionals, verbal or written announcements at conferences and agencywide gatherings, specific announcements to health providers, special newsletters, word of mouth, and client referrals. Because the diagnosis of AIDS carries the risk of stigma and discrimination, announcements of or referrals to such a group should be handled in a manner that ensures confidentiality (Dhooper and Royse, 1989; O'Rourke and Sutherland, 1994). The provision of services to PWAs in rural settings (Anderson and Shaw, 1994; Rounds, 1988; Rounds, Galinsky, and Stevens, 1991; Drucker, 1992) illustrates how to obtain group membership while maintaining strict confidentiality. In one such rural setting, a facilitator was able to introduce the concept of a PWA support group through an article in the town newspaper. She was then able to screen members by phone and obtain a commitment to confidentiality among prospective group members prior to the initial group meeting, which was conducted in the facilitator's home. Such safeguards to confidentiality need to be initiated in almost every setting where HIV/AIDS groups are being planned. Techniques such as using first names, relying heavily on telephone contact, not identifying how one has come to know a particular member, and eliminating recording of personal data about each member also contribute to protecting members' anonymity. Of course, it is understood that agencies have clearly delineated procedures about recording group attendance. However, facilitators are obligated to address these charting requirements in a way that protects the members' confidentiality, i.e., by not recording the specifics of a member's reaction to his or her illness, and not revealing family name, location, situation, or relationship to others. Recording the process, attendance, and emotional or physical status of a member is often all that is required.

BOUNDARIES FOR SUPPORT GROUPS: PLACE, TIME, SIZE, AND OUT-OF-GROUP CONTACT

Boundaries for support groups are operationally defined by such dimensions as place, time, size, attendance, and agreements regarding out-of-group contact between members. For groups whose mission is to provide mutual aid, empowerment, and reconnection in the face of traumatizing stressors, boundaries tend to be more permeable and less rigid. Many of these parameters—place, time, size, attendance, and out-of-group contacts—must be negotiated from the perspective of the group's history and current themes defining or fueling the group processes. Unlike other group psychotherapies that comprise persons whose primary focus is on character change and symptom reduction, the approach in support group therapy is more flexible and responsive to the group's direction. Thus, a group may change its time, move from one space to another (for example, from a group room to a hospital room or to a member's home for a period of time), and even enlarge its size by inviting a small number of new members into the group. These accommodations to the group's wishes should be undertaken only after exploration and when it is clear that there is a consensus or compromise and no adamant objections from any group member. Such flexibility is essential if the group is to be helped to tolerate, manage, and to some degree master the uncertainties and anxieties that threaten their sense of empowerment.

Space

Within the confines of physical space, group members, with their facilitators' assistance, need to create a "safe refuge" wherein the narratives of the trauma of HIV/AIDS may be constructed in ways that permit healing. This is accomplished primarily through bridging (Ormont, 1992b). While the concept of boundaries is always an important consideration in group work, it takes on a particular importance or meaning in groups with traumatized persons, who for a variety of reasons have been overwhelmed by either physical or emotional events and/or information. Essentially the boundaries of traumatized persons have been violated. For the PWA, space represents an important boundary symbolic of the PWA's wish to be located along the continuum of this illness. For example, some of the questions posed by PWAs reflecting their concerns about location (in other words, "Where am I"?), "How sick am I?" "Am I as sick as she is?" "What will the next infection be?" and "How close to death am I?" Since its identification, HIV has been discussed as a "continuum" illness: first HIV infection, then, one hopes, a period of time without significant symptoms, then the development of a major opportunistic infection or a drop in t-cells, constituting a diagnosis of AIDS. Those persons whose viral infection does not progress are referred to as "nonprogressors."

In practical ways, the space place chosen for such groups should be accessible to the physically and visually challenged. It should be well cared for. Rooms with dirty chairs, over-flowing wastebaskets, and poor ventilation reinforce feelings of being "overwhelmed" and "out of control." It is very im-portant, given the increasing reports of tuberculosis and mul-tiple-drug-resistant tuberculosis (MDRTB) in the HIV popu-lation (Riley, 1993) to ensure that the space offers adequate health protection to members and facililators. Group mem-bers and facilitators with already compromised immune sys-tems need well-ventilated rooms. If such cannot be obtained, there needs to be ongoing dialogue in the group about the "risk" nature of the group room and the actions or steps needed to be taken to secure more protected space.

In these circumstances, thoughts of contagion and the wearing or not wearing of a TB mask for protection from all exposure to airborne bacteria may be constantly on the minds of both members and facilitators. And like the proverbial "ele-phant in the room," it is an issue that fills the space but re-mains unaddressed in direct ways. Members and facilitators often share a sense of shame or fear regarding verbalizing their worries over physical contagion. Field and Shore (1992), writing on their three years of experience with a PWA group, reflect on their unspoken fears of physical contagion:

> For a time the authors found physical contact with the pa-
> tient, those handshakes and hugs, so necessary to the comfort-
> ing of the seriously ill, uncomfortable. Before starting the

group we had even procured a supply of disinfectant for hand-washing after each session. Our anxiety faded as experience and education helped us differentiate real dangers from irrational concerns, just as it has for most professionals. For us, the denouement came at a party for the first anniversary of our group when a patient asked if we would eat what he had baked. (p. 161)

It is difficult when the facilitators harbor feelings of unacceptance about such concerns. This phenomenon parallels the increased fear of rape, or violence, reported by rape counselors and therapists who work with survivors of violence (Pearlman and Saakvitne, 1995)—feelings induced both by the reality of the situation and through association with traumatized persons.

Thus issues of space provide numerous opportunities to address the array of special issues related to groups with AIDS. A group room should provide members and facilitators with a choice of seat within a circle. Chairs should be carefully arranged with the expectation of all members' arrival. Thus, if the facilitators have a roster of twelve members, then twelve chairs should be available. Chairs are often provided for absent members, symbolizing that absence from the group does not mean termination. It also provides a way of remembering a member who is not present. In such instances members and facilitators may refer to the absent member whose presence is signified by the chair. Of course, this symbolic gesture may be burdensome and contraindicated when empty chairs outnumber occupied chairs, and the chairs of absent members come to dominate the group space. At these times, the group often makes some decision about how to manage the empty chairs, knowing full well that such an "empty chair" may be a portent of their own future.

One group facilitator reported that he and his co-facilitator asked their group if the empty chairs inhibited, enhanced or had no effect on them. These leaders found that despite some members' indifference, each seemed to feel that being "remembered" in this way helped them to feel connected to the group when they were away. One said, "I sometimes imagine from the hospital bed that you are all saving a place for me."

Time and Attendance

A less tangible parameter than space, but perhaps the most important for members of PWA support groups, is time. Because time is the most precious commodity when one is confronting illness or the threat of death, violations of the time boundary in these groups is always significant, e.g., not coming, late coming, leaving early, choosing to attend to another commitment instead of being in group on time. And it is more often than not a communication to the group about the group, the group process, group facilitation, the member's external life, and/or the member's internal life. These instances require careful exploration by facilitators and members. In beginning sessions it is too great a demand to expect members to address such matters directly with other members. Facilitators need to model for members ways in which to explore group resistances without attacking. In some instances, through such exploration usually in the first few sessions, group members discover that other stressors may need more attention at this time than their AIDS diagnosis:

A member in her fourth session in a PWA support group talked about how the group was having a "negative" effect on her and her recovery from alcohol addiction. She explained that she could not tolerate the "death talk" and "all this doctor talk." What she needed was help to stay "sober." Her sobriety was to her the major goal since it involved possible reunion with her children. At the conclusion of her articulated assessment, which initially sounded like an attack on the group, the members responded that she should be in the kind of group that was the most helpful. Perhaps even in two groups—this one and another for her recovery. She thought it a fine idea and responded that she would come to this group when "my t-cells can take this death talk."

The freedom to leave the group, especially after a few initial sessions, or to come to a PWA group in addition to another kind of support group, fuels members' sense of empowerment and enhances their support network. This flexibility and openness are central to trauma recovery. When a group has been planned to incorporate members' other stressors, e.g., poverty, stigma, chemical dependency, lack of access to entitlements and health services, then absences or irregularity in attendance, especially after the first twelve sessions, may have more to do with group dynamics, particularly if this "fragmentation" in the support group occurs after a number of hospitalizations or deaths.

The notion of a member's attendance or time contract with the group emerged from studies of "drop-out" phenomena done by Yalom and his colleagues (Lothstein, 1978; McCallum, Piper, and Joyce, 1992; Stone, Blase, and Bozzuto, 1980; Stone and Rutan, 1984; Yalom, 1966). The findings of these studies suggest that members by the twelfth session have established a relationship with other group members if they are going to. After this time period they are less likely to leave the group. For many facilitators this has translated into the "twelve-session contract" period. In many instances facilitators in PWA support groups (Field and Shore, 1992; Beckett and Rutan, 1990) have asked for a shorter initial contract, since cohesiveness in such trauma groups appears to develop more rapidly. It seems for some members the urgency of time plays a major role in their expectations of these groups. For example, when a facilitator of a women-with-AIDS group asked the group, early in its life, what the group thought about the way the group had been spending its time, some members complained bitterly. They reported feeling the group should focus more on life issues instead of death issues. This led to a discussion of how time was passing too quickly for them and how they were feeling pressure to live more in the present and worry less about the future.

This theme of living in the present is an important ingredient in support groups with PWAs, because the future is so uncertain and filled with many terrors. Often, for some, the trauma associated with the past as well as the future renders the present more comforting. The support group becomes a space where members are able to indulge in the "consciousness of being" (Heideggar, 1962) and ushers in a host of existential concerns, i.e., basic isolation, capriciousness of existence, and recognition of mortality. In most instances group time and the group's work is in the "here and now," focused on some what have been termed existential factors (Yalom, 1995), with members journeying into their past and past relationships at crucial intervals while concentrating on current concerns, usually health-related.

Group Size and Its Fluctuations

In a sense, size and attendance issues provide metaphors for this disease and its sequelae. In group practice, groups are thought to function best when they are closed, i.e., limited to five or six members. Support groups, on the other hand, range in size from the traditional five or six to ten to twelve members (Adams, 1979; Burke, Coddington, Bakeman, and Clance, 1994). For AIDS support groups where all members share one common stressor—an AIDS diagnosis and life-threatening illness—the recommended size is ten to twelve or more, depending on the overall health of the group (Field and Shore, 1992; Norsworthy and Horne, 1994; Gabriel, 1991; Sageman, 1989; Tunnell, 1991, 1994). In a group in which most of the membership are physically deteriorated, it is important to maintain a sufficient number of attending members. In this way the facilitators and members may entertain a broader range of life issues, including major health-related concerns. More important, size and attendance are crucial in defining the role of the facilitators, because they may be quickly identified as the only healthy and constant persons in the group. As Tunnel (1991) observed:

> Because the group's membership is so unstable at certain times, the strongest bond will likely be between each member and the therapist. . . . it is important that the therapist not resort to doing multiple individual therapies during group sessions. Again, the therapist must be mindful of group process, attempt-

ing to understand whatever is happening that is interfering with members helping one another. (p. 488)

Even with an expanded roster of members, attendance fluctuates greatly in these groups, and inconsistency in attendance reflects the major feature of this illness, i.e., its unpredictable course. Facilitators need to keep in mind that attendance, especially in the formative stages of the group—the first three to four months—may be punctuated by many absences and lateness.

Given that PWAs often have a multiple of stressors, the facilitators understand group resistances within the conceptual framework of persons with multiple traumas. PWAs may be detached, apathetic, and often depressed as a response to the trauma of diagnosis or illness, or as a response to their overall life situations. Facilitators may anticipate their own distress, disappointment, and even rage at members for their inconsistent and sometimes habitual absences. More than any other factor, the absent member syndrome appears to contribute the most to facilitators' discouragement and hopelessness around the formation and maintenance of these support groups. As the group size diminishes through hospitalizations, illnesses, and deaths, absence for any reason may become a reminder of loss and the continuing threat of death. Given the nature of trauma from life-threatening illness and the helplessness and disempowerment that may accompany it, it is understandable, perhaps even to be expected, that members convey an unsettling detachment from and disinterest in the facilitators. When this occurs, facilitators may respond by attempting to "take charge" of the group, thereby inadvertently disempowering it.

New Members

For those facilitating a PWA group, it is important to have some way of encouraging new membership and maintaining a workable group size, wherein members are sufficient in number to provide mutual aid. Given the frequent absences due to illness, related events, or demands related to psychosocial stressors, maintaining a core group is likely to occupy an enormous portion of the facilitator's time and energy. If at all possible, group facilitators may want to maintain a list of fourteen to sixteen prospective members or a referral source that gives them access to new members in order to assure core membership. Membership in the group is likely to vacillate between a full complement to at times a handful. When only a few members are present, empty chairs may represent a threat both to the individual and to the integrity of the group. Group size then takes on enormous meaning, raising such concerns in members as who will get sick next. It is a time when members and facilitators grapple with the existential meaning of life, attempting to deal with its capriciousness and uncertainty.

To circumvent these issues, members often focus on their wish to add new members, i.e., "new blood." The new blood metaphor appears to have symbolic meaning to ill members, who view the survival of the group as some way of maintaining hope and keeping their memory alive should they die, i.e., "the group holds the memory." Adding new blood not only speaks to the dynamics of hope and continuity but to the altruism of group members as well:

In one PWA group which had continued for five years, all but one original member had died. A number of new members had been added through the years. In speaking of new members, the one surviving member observed that new members in groups like these are equal to a "transfusion," bringing to them "new life." With regard to new members, he said, "newies" mean that "maybe what I have been through will have some meaning to others. Maybe I have something to give . . . Maybe this hell can be avoided by others, especially the 'stupid' things, like not telling anyone until I got very sick, etc."

Although periods of closed membership are crucial, especially during time of crises, e.g., death of member, sudden hospitalization, or suicide of a member, when the size diminishes, the focus on grieving may outlive its therapeutic benefit. Remaining members who face a similar fate may need distraction, i.e., relief from the reality of illness and multiple deaths. The fact that "man cannot bear too much reality" is something that facilitators need to respect in supporting and protecting the life of the group.

On one cold winter evening ten out of fifteen members came to group. This was the first time in months that more than five members were present. With the ten members present there was a lightness, an optimism not before seen in this group. There was talk of fantasy vacations to sunny places, shared laughter, stories of embarrassing moments told with bravado, and in general, future oriented stories devoid of any mention of illness. When the facilitators asked what accounted for the mood of the group, one member observed that there were more members present, which evoked a sense of relief. "We have survived another week and we are together, right here and now."

In contrast is the small-group session, where the membership has been considerably reduced in size as a consequence of several deaths all occurring within a six-month period.

In this group the facilitators felt that the group might not survive the deaths of so many members. The sense of grief and mourning had become overwhelming. The group seemed withdrawn and distant with silences punctuating most attempts to talk with one other. Two of the members in fact considered leaving the group for fear that the group would not be able to help them stay alive.

What appears most important in facilitating a group at this juncture is each member's capacity to locate the pain involved in such connection to others. Such connection involves maintaining hope while dealing with loss.

Enhancement of Group Attendance

One way to address some of the obstacles to attendance by group members—I have an important diagnostic test tomorrow and need to prepare myself; I can't come to group because I am feeling fatigued and may have a fever; I can't come because I may have a drug reaction since I started new medications; I can't come because the group time conflicts with my doctor's appointment; I can't come because my child care fell through—is to explore the importance of the event to the member and determine whether the member can accomplish both the external task as well as attend the group. In support group therapy the underlying principle is empowerment. Thus, exploration needs to induce empowerment in members if it is to be therapeutic.

A member of a group which had been meeting for several months called to say she would not be coming because she was fatigued. When this was explored by the facilitator, what emerged was the member's fear of the side effects of her new medication, particularly the fear that it might cause her to "fall asleep" in the group. The facilitator suggested she come to the group to present her dilemma as well as to find out how the group would feel if she fell asleep and how they might help her stay awake. The fatigue was, of course, only one of a series of concerns that she had about the new medications.

In another group, a member called to say he could not come because he was "too mentally weak" and hearing others complain and be depressed might only weaken him further. In exploring the issue of his emotional weakness—How is the weakness affecting you? How will it get worse in the group? Is there something the group can do to help you with this emotional weakness?—the facilitator came to realize that the major concern was about his escalating depressive thoughts. The facilitator encouraged the member to talk with the group about these thoughts, since many other group members had struggled with similar thoughts and experiences.

Basically, the goal of all the facilitators' interventions in these vignettes entailed enabling members to attend the group despite their fears and resistances, suggesting that the group would provide an accepting and empowering environment. Facilitators need to keep in mind that the most debilitating consequence of the trauma of a life-threatening illness such as AIDS is that it isolates the group member. Such isolation may become as traumatic as many of the symptoms of the illness itself, thus negatively affecting the overall health and well-being of a member.

Members' Relationship to Each Other Outside the Group

In contrast to other group therapies, support group therapy makes no rules about members' relationships outside of group. In fact, support group facilitators often encourage members to contact and speak with one another outside the weekly ninety-minute sessions. Building on the rationale of mutual aid, comfort, and support, such connections are essentially viewed as strengthening the members' support network and heightening reconnection. However, group practitioners need to be mindful of the problems inherent in outside group contact, since the formation of dyads or tryads may develop, leading to greater interest in these subgroups than in the group as whole. This may result in a member's diminished interest in participating in group or, in some circumstances, abandonment of the group. Even given these potential pitfalls, however, support groups with PWAs where the course of the illness is both unpredictable and potentially debilitating, members need a safety net, including other members with whom they have more frequent contact. A seven-day interim between group meetings may be experienced by a group member as torturous, especially a member who is particularly isolated or overwhelmed with fears and worries. And a more prolonged separation from group for a member because of illness or hospitalization may be experienced as even more distressing. One member spoke of the importance of his out-of-group contact with members following a brief absence from his group due to hospitalization for an AIDS-related infection:

> I took my list of phone numbers [group members] with me. I wanted you all to call and if none of you did, I was going to call you all [laughs]. Glad I didn't have to reach out and touch you. But I would have. My roommate was calling and getting calls from his family in Iowa. And I had my family . . . you all! And I know everything that's been going on in here [group], so watch out—, Ed is back in person!

Summary

This chapter focused on those issues related to the formation of support groups for PWAs. Addressed were such issues as membership, group dynamics, co-facilitation, and group goals. With regard to membership, special consideration was given to the difficulties encountered by chemically dependent women in obtaining social supports especially in the form of an AIDS support group. Boundaries for such support groups—especially place, time, and size—were addressed with special emphasis on the symbolic meaning of time and space to the PWA. Size of group was discussed as a particularly complex aspect of such groups, especially in light of the unpredictable course of AIDS and its associated stigma. Several clinical vignettes were provided which further explicated the issue of group size and the complexities involved in introducing new members into AIDS support groups. This chapter provided an overview of the structural differences between the traditional therapeutic group and the AIDS support group.

CHAPTER 3

Special Issues and Considerations in Support Groups with PWAs

Confidentiality, Dementia, TB, Rational Suicide, and Multiple Deaths

A number of special issues and considerations arise in support groups with PWAs. Consideration will be given here only to those issues most frequently encountered and reported upon both in the literature on support groups for PWAs and in group supervision sessions. Special issues and considerations include confidentiality in group, the member in the group with dementia, the member with tuberculosis and/or multiple-drug-resistant tuberculosis (MDRTB), the suicidal member, and the issue of rational suicide and the impact of multiple deaths of members on the group.

ISSUES OF CONFIDENTIALITY IN PWA SUPPORT GROUPS

Protecting a member's confidentiality in group therapies has always been a challenge. Legal safeguards for confidentiality in group modalities are weaker than for individual therapies (Appelbaum and Greer, 1993; Davis and Meara, 1982; Kearney, 1984; Gregory and McConnell, 1986; Miller and Thelen, 1987). The sheer number of persons present in any group endeavor increases the risk of leaks or dissemination of information. The applicability of psychotherapy patient privilege communication status to group therapy is questionable in most states (Smith, 1986, in Appelbaum and Greer, 1993). Courts have long held that the presence of third parties in group therapies compromises the circumstances under which privileged communication can be invoked, although some courts have extended the privilege to cover communications made to or in the presence of a person assisting the psychotherapist with diagnosis or treatment. This provides a rationale for viewing the group participants as part of the treatment team (Appelbaum and Greer, 1993; Buie, 1989).

The results of a recent study (Roback, Ochoa, Bloch, and Purdon, 1992) suggest that group practitioners recognize confidentiality as vital to therapeutic outcome in group therapies and believe, as well, that groups are at greater risk for breaches than other psychotherapeutic endeavors. Investigators in this study reported that the group practitioners always informed prospective group members of the confidentiality limitations, discussed issues of confidentiality during the first group session, but found existing guidelines for confidentiality within groups as not helpful. They agreed that a clear legal definition of what constituted group confidentiality and its limits was needed. Given these observations, support group facilitators need to pay particular attention to issues of confidentiality, in part because of the difficulties inherent in achieving confidentiality, especially in an atmosphere of group crisis and inconsistent membership. While confidentiality may be a major issue in any group therapy[1] setting, it carries a certain sense of urgency within AIDS support groups, perhaps because for some the information shared in AIDS support groups or the knowledge of being in such a group may be highly stigmatizing information (Herek and Glunt, 1988). Such information, if disseminated in the community, may result in a member's exclusion from relationships, employment, and/or health care.

Confidentiality both as an ethical standard and as a legal protection in support group therapy represents a boundary symbolizing the safety and protection a person seeks in joining such groups. A support group is often viewed as a place where the PWA can reveal a range of thoughts, feelings, and actions associated with coping with this illness and associated stressors. Traditionally in AIDS groups, confidentiality is negotiated from early on, beginning with the prescreening interview. Concerns about confidentiality are more often articulated indirectly in PWA groups, often expressed through a member's questions about greeting another member should they run into each other outside the group, about how or whether to leave a telephone or e-mail message for another member, or how to respond to a group member's family and friends at the hospital. Seldom do the group members or facilitators talk directly about the complex issues of confidentiality or the circumstances under which a member's confidentiality may be breached (Posey, 1988). Interestingly, worries about exposure leading to rejection by significant others and the conspiracy of silence born of this lingering concern continue to exert their influence, even within the relative safety of the group. Thus it is of paramount importance that group facilitators work to make the indirect direct.

Full disclosure is thought to fuel the processes of healing, especially for persons who have been traumatized. Imagine a Vietnam veterans' support group where the members could not fully disclose the atrocities they participated in and/or witnessed for fear of public disclosure or criminal indictment. Or a rape support group where a rape survivor talks of being able to identify the rapist, refuses to, and asks the group members and facilitators not to intervene with authorities on her behalf because of her fear of shame, public disclosure, and possible retaliation.

The sanctity of confidentiality between client and practitioner has been a paramount principle for all the mental health professions. Psychiatry, psychology, and social work have considered it to be a central ethical principle in their associations' codes of ethics (American Psychiatry Association, American Psychological Association, and National Association of Social Workers). Confidentiality appears central to the effectiveness of certain psychological models of treatment such as psychoanalysis, where clients are asked to "say everything," "talk freely," or "tell the story of their life."

Breaches of confidentiality can occur in two contexts: when the individual or group practitioner or group members are subpoenaed to testify in court and when practitioners or group members reveal information they have learned in group sessions to a third party, either intentionally or as an implementation of the Tarasoff doctrine, i.e., the duty to "protect" third parties.

In view of the centrality of confidentiality in the arena of psychological interventions, it is not surprising that the current dilemmas arising out of the exceptions to absolute confidentiality have prompted such rigorous and sometime vociferous debate. In the HIV environment, what is critical to the current debate and legislative activity may be understood in the form of a question: Must a clinician violate confidentiality when a client is known to be HIV-infected and is sexually active or sharing needles with partners who are unaware of the client's infection? (Lamb, Clark, Drumheller, Frizzell, and Surrey, 1989).

Tarasoff Doctrine and HIV/AIDS-Related Psychotherapies

Until the Tarasoff doctrine in 1974, the "duty to warn" and later extended to the "duty to protect" third parties (California State Supreme Court, 1976) was a form of absolute confidentiality extended to most psychotherapies. The exceptions were the mandatory protection laws focused on protection of children as the third parties (Reamer, 1991). The Tarasoff doctrine, coupled with the emergence of the AIDS-pandemic, precipitated a conflict between the rights of third parties who may be at risk because of their sexual relationship or needle-sharing relationship with persons with AIDS. This struggle has taken center stage in literature related to issues of confidentiality and ethical responsibility in AIDS-related psychotherapy (Erickson, 1993; Gray and Harding, 1988; Hughes and Friedman, 1994; Kain, 1988; Kermani and Weiss, 1989; Lamb, Clark, Drumheller, Frizzell, and Surrey, 1989; Morrison, 1989; Melton, 1988; Reamer, 1991; Totten, Lamb, and Reeder, 1990; Yu and O'Neal, 1992). Essentially the Tarasoff doctrine has become a general legal reference point for licensed mental health professionals, e.g., psychiatrists, psychologists, and social workers, in establishing parameters of confidentiality. In what is now a famous case, an out-patient of the University of California Hospital revealed in his psychotherapy treatment the intent to harm his ex-girlfriend, Tatiana Tarasoff. The practitioner notified the police of this man's intention but failed to warn the potential victim. Two months later this man shot and killed Tarasoff. In its precedent-setting decision, the California Supreme Court recognized a new form of negligence and ruled that the therapist had failed to exercise reasonable care in protecting a potential victim. This case more than any other forged the landscape for contemporary debate about the limits of clients' right to confidentiality and mental health professionals' duty to protect third parties.

Three conditions need to be met before considering application of the Tarasoff doctrine to any situation involving breach of confidentiality on the basis of duty to protect: a special relationship must exist, there must be some perceived danger, and the intended victim in need of protection must be identifiable. Those who write about the application of the Tarasoff doctrine in certain HIV-specific psychotherapy situations suggest that in certain instances these conditions are, indeed, met (Erickson, 1993; Gray and Harding, 1988; Knapp and VandeCreek, 1990; Lamb, Clark, Drumheller, Frizzell, and Surrey, 1989). The argument is that the relationship between the client and mental health professional appears to satisfy the criteria of a special relationship (Lamb, Clark, Drumheller, Frizzell, and Surrey, 1989). With regard to dangerousness, the debate becomes complex, because it is not AIDS per se that is transmitted but the virus associated with it (HIV). Since the point at which an individual becomes HIV-seropositive or develops HIV symptoms cannot be predicted, nor is every unprotected sexual encounter or needle sharing

experience sure to lead to infection, the degree of dangerousness criteria becomes more obscure (Knapp and VandeCreek,
1990; Melton, 1988). With regard to the third condition,
identifiable victim, the Tarasoff ruling (California State
Supreme Court, 1976) clearly states:

> once the therapist does in fact determine, or . . . should have
> determined, that a patient poses a serious danger of violence to
> others, he bears a duty to exercise reasonable care to protect the
> foreseeable victim of that danger. (p. 335)

There appears to be legal direction and ethical standards
that dictate that in certain instances the mental health professional in HIV-related psychotherapy practices involving both
individual and group modalities bears some responsibility for
protection of third parties from possible harm from HIV-in-
fection. What is important in this, however, is that the California Supreme Court ruling emphasized protection, not duty
to warn. Thus, protection of an identifiable victim may be
achieved without breach of an individual's or a group member's confidentiality. All the literature in this area cautions the
practitioner to use a variety of other methods to limit the risk
to third parties, with breach of confidentiality of the PWA as
an extreme and last resort.

Implications for AIDS Support Groups

Thus support group therapy for people with AIDS usually
takes place in an environment that is complex and replete
with ethical and clinical concerns and dilemmas. As such, a
variety of situations present themselves to the group practitioner which may involve the questions of protection of iden-

tifiable third parties. The following group vignette illustrates some of the dilemmas encountered by group practitioners in such support groups.

Milly has been in an AIDS support group for three months. She is distraught because a man whom she was dating left her once he learned she had AIDS. She tells the group that she has no intention of ever telling another lover again. She expresses her intention instead to go out and find a man who can give her a child before she dies. It is clear to the group that Milly is currently having high risk sex and some members perceive her as intentionally attempting to transmit the virus.

One man in the group responded to Milly by gesturing dismissingly to her, saying, "keep away from me, you're one sick lady!"

Another member responded by asking, "What's got you so angry? So you got dumped, people get dumped every day. They don't go out and try to kill a bunch of unsuspecting guys. What is your problem, Milly?

The group members continued this dialogue and at one point the facilitators wondered aloud whether or not someone should be warning people in the community that Milly was a danger, maybe even report her to public health authorities for spreading the virus. This exploration led Milly to talk about how these were somewhat idle threats because since the breakup she has not been having sex because it scares her to think she might get pregnant. All her anger, doubts and disappointments about not having had children emerged within the group, resulting in a response of empathy and understanding from other group members.

Obviously this was the "best scenario" at this moment for Milly in this group. The process and the group's reactions plus the facilitator's explorations allowed her an opportunity to "hear herself." In this instance, obviously there is no specific identifiable victim. If there were, it would be most important to help Milly address the behaviors rather than for the facilitator or group members to breach her confidentiality to do so. In support group, the facilitators have the help of group members in trying to assist members in controlling behaviors that may be destructive to themselves and others. As often happens in group, an individual member's respective emotional style of responding and communicating, i.e., angry, sympathetic, indifferent, empathetic, usually captures some aspect of other members' feelings. Milly, in response to her feelings of abandonment, would initially only conjure up feelings of revenge. Having her vengeful wishes labeled by group members permitted her to examine these threats and experience other feelings and emotions more directly.

Most troublesome and professionally tumultuous for group facilitators and group members are instances where a group member is not only someone dying of AIDS but also in the grips of acting out rage associated with the unabated progression of the disease. In these instances the group as a whole begins to feel implicated in the PWA's intention to harm.

Ben had been a member of an AIDS support group for two years. During this time his condition steadily deteriorated. Despite his determination to live with AIDS, he was dying. He left his job, went on disability, moved in with an old lover/friend and began to spend more time and energy attending to his illness, doctor's appointments, infusion therapy, stress workshops, etc. A few months ago Ben met and "fell in love with" an old friend who was also diagnosed HIV but was asymptomatic. Ben shared all this with the group, and was for the first time in months energized and hopeful. After a few weeks, Ben discovered that his new love, who was now living with him, was also involved in another relationship, with a woman, whom he had once been married to. Ben felt completely desolate in his response to this discovery. First depressed then enraged, feeling abandoned and betrayed, he told the group of his intention to willfully infect as many people as possible before he died. His rage coupled with these threats was unusual for Ben, who had always appeared a rather passive, thoughtful, nonvengeful person. The group responded to Ben by becoming "paralyzed" and nonreactive.

In the subsequent session, Ben continued to be openly rageful. When asked if he intended to willfully have "sex," he said flatly, "nothing has changed." The members pointed out that "this was murder." Some tried to investigate his motives. Others commented on how unlike him this was, and that he had changed dramatically in the last few weeks. The facilitators asked, why should the group aid and abet murder? This led to a group discussion of the various measures that could be taken to prohibit Ben from acting on these intentions. Members devised various plans: shared responsibility for spending time with him, locking him in his apartment, following him when he goes out, posting a notice telling others of his intention, etc. The group's discussion of limit taking actions, as unrealistic as they might appear, provided Ben with some relief and ultimately allowed him to express his overwhelming depression and despair about the prospect of dying alone. Once his feelings of depression were identified, members were able to convince him to seek a psychological support in addition to the group.

Ben ultimately obtained a therapist recommended by one of

the group members, a step which enhanced Ben's commitment to the group and theirs to him.

Taken collectively, group confidentiality is an extremely complicated norm to establish and maintain in support group therapy for people with AIDS. Its importance is monumental in comparison with all other elements of group process, since violations of confidentiality may likely be destructive to the group. When confidentiality is breached and a member's diagnosis, illness, and behaviors surrounding the virus become public knowledge, it is difficult for a group to recapture the trust or cohesiveness needed for it to be maintained. Ultimately the group's safety has been undermined, and for some this kind of intrusion cannot be healed without a recognition of the ultimate retraumatization that has taken place.

SPECIAL CONSIDERATION: THE DEMENTED MEMBER

In 1987, recognizing the prevalence and severity of HIV-related neurological dysfunction, the Centers for Disease Control added AIDS Dementia Complex to its roster of AIDS-defining disorders. The most common form of this disorder is HIV-associated dementia complex (HADC). Clinical manifestations of HADC are subtle and have an insidious onset, with forgetfulness and loss of concentration as the most frequently cited early symptoms (Navia and Price, 1987). Descriptively, PWAs diagnosed with dementia complain of attention difficulties, memory problems, confusion, and mental slowing. Attention lapses may be manifested in the inability to read a book; difficulty in following a television program or directions; problems sustaining a conversation; trouble paying attention to several different interchanges in conversations; difficulty remembering how to operate mechanisms and devices, e.g., microwaves, computers, television sets. Those close to a person with AIDS dementia may observe and report withdrawal, agitation, anxiety, irritability, and personality changes (Beckett and Kassel, 1994). Subtle cognitive and affective complaints often parallel the symptoms of major depression. Kassel (1990) suggests the presence of motor impairments when no other neurological illnesses are evidenced, an important symptom in making the diagnosis between clinical psychiatric illness such as major depression and dementia, since motor impairments are extremely rare in most psychiatric illnesses. Currently, there is no cure for HADC, but psychopharmacological and other therapeutic interventions may substantially alter the course of the illness or provide significant relief for some of the symptoms. Pharmacologic treatments include zidovudine (AZT) or increasing the dosage in patients who are already on such medications, use of psychostimulants such as methylphenidate (Ritalin) or dextroamphetamine (Dexedrine) (Beckett and Kassel, 1994; Levy, Bredesen, and Rosenblum, 1985; Lunn, Skydsbjerg, and Schulsinger, 1991).

Group facilitators and members alike need to struggle in understanding and deciphering a member's situation when beginning dementia is suspected. Is a member primarily depressed or are the symptoms suggestive of a primary diagnosis of dementias? Are the members aware of these changes? What is the member's response and manner of coping? Whatever the case, the member may use the group to talk about these changes while the group may encourage the member not only to talk but to explore the situation with a physician. Members' observations regarding the demented and/or depressed member constitute a level of witnessing that may be traumatizing, because the presence of this member makes real what may be the members' worst fantasy.

The course of HADC is highly variable. In some instances there may be little or no progression of deficits, and the PWA may develop mechanisms for coping with them. Group members who have some deficits often talk with others about their methods of coping, which often include making lists, color-coding different items, posting signs, using mechanical devices to signal when certain tasks should take place, and labeling different drawers and files (Levy, Bredesen, and Rosenblum, 1985; Tross and Hirsch, 1988).

Even though members who have dementia may not be fully aware of the changes they are experiencing, other members are usually acutely aware and need numerous opportunities to talk about the effect on them. The complexity of the issues related to the onset of dementia in a group member and its impact on group processes is illustrated in the following example.

Dave had been in the PWA support group for six years. He was an articulate, friendly, humorous man, whom the group was very much attached to despite his noticeably controlling manner. Dave's style of interacting made it almost impossible for anyone to be "helpful" to him, although he was quite adamant about his willingness and ability to help others. Dave, considered by the group to be the "Gay poster boy," was diagnosed with AIDS in the early 1980s and was determined to be a "long-term survivor." As each OI [opportunistic infection] threatened his determination, Dave became even more convinced that he would survive long enough for a cure. In his sixth year in the group, Dave began showing symptoms of confusion, [and was] sometimes unable to follow conversations in the group or provide relevant feed-back, which suggested that he had either not been listening, had misunderstood or was courting some illness. It soon became clear that something was wrong cognitively. One session when Dave was absent a member raised the issue of changes in Dave, an issue that the group including the facilitators had been avoiding. Of course, every member had some thought and their own rendition of what was "wrong with Dave." Their respective worst fears about their own situations were poignantly articulated.

These opportunities to talk about what was wrong with Dave, both with Dave present and in his absence, gave the group an opportunity not only to make conscious and begin to process their own worries, but to rally around Dave just as a family would rally around a sick member. Dave, of course, true to his character, continued to believe more often than not that he was his old self, still providing helpful advice to others.

Whatever the case for Dave, his presence in the group, and the presence of PWAs with dementia in support groups, is potentially both traumatizing and healing for group members. Members frequently articulate as their worst fear becoming demented, the fear of being abandoned and left to die alone, bedridden, in pain, and out of their minds (Rabkin, Remien, and Wilson, 1994). Participating in a group where the members "take care" of each other in the face of hardships, such as a member's dementia, can in the best of circumstances contribute to a sense of cohesiveness, a sense that in these groups, the members will have a place, an identity, a history despite mental and physical deterioration.

THE MEMBER WITH TUBERCULOSIS AND
MULTIPLE-DRUG-RESISTANT TB

Tuberculosis, once the leading cause of death in the United States in the late nineteenth century, has resurfaced as a major public health problem in the United States (Hopewell, 1992; Castro, Valdiserri, and Curran, 1992). The deterioration of the public health infrastructure along with inadequate training of health care providers in the epidemiology of tuberculosis are some of the factors contributing to the increased incidence of TB. Those living in large urban areas, in inadequate housing, and in poverty conditions and those with HIV/AIDS are particularly vulnerable. For those with HIV who develop tuberculosis, the morality rates reach 80% in 2 to 3 months postdiagnosis (Barnes and Barrows, 1993). Contributing to this morality rate is death from an iatrogenic form of tuberculosis, multiple drug-resistant tuberculosis (MDRTB), a form which evolves from inadequate diagnosis and/or incomplete treatment of the tuberculosis. When TB treatment is interrupted, it allows mutation in the organisms to occur that produces a drug resistant TB microbe (Riley, 1993; Fella, Rivera, Sepkowitz, Hale, and Ramos, 1992). Tuberculosis poses a particular threat to those with compromised immune systems, and it is an issue which evokes considerable concern and distress in group members when introduced into the life of an AIDS support group either because a member has TB or has been exposed to TB.

Tuberculosis is an infectious disease caused by a microorganism known as *Mycobacterium tuberculosis*. It most commonly infects the lungs, causing a persistent cough, weight loss, fever, night sweats, and fatigue. In some instances, such as in PWAs or persons with HIV, TB may involve extrapulmonary sites, such as the lymphatic or genitourinary systems, or other body organs and tissues. It is generally transmitted by coughing, sneezing, and talking, activities that release the microbe into a given environment. People with acute TB expel microscopic droplets of bacteria from their lungs or throats that can linger for hours in uncirculated air. Except in specially designated areas designed to address the spread of TB known as negative pressure areas, most group practice rooms, for example, are without circulating air, thereby increasing the risk of TB, especially for immune-compromised persons. While a person with a healthy immune system may breathe contaminated air for months before becoming infected, the probability of serious infection soars when a person's immune system is weakened and flourishes in those who have already existing opportunistic infections, such as PWAs. A further complication for PWAs is that TB is often more difficult to diagnose in people with HIV disease. The general diagnostic tools, e.g., Mantoux tuberculin skin test or PPD skin test, chest X rays, and anergy tests, are difficult to read and are sometimes misinterpreted in people with HIV. An even more disturbing occurrence particularly affecting the HIV community and those with AIDS is the rise of MDRTB. With this form of TB, the organisms have become resistant to at least one and often more than one drug used in treatment (New York State Department of Health AIDS Institute, 1993; Kilborn, 1994). Timely diagnosis of MDRTB is necessary, but often the drug-susceptibility tests are delayed and the person with MDRTB remains sick. Ultimately the person grows sicker, unaware of the deadly nature of this disease and, simultaneously and unknowingly, exposes other group members, whose immune systems are also compromised.

When the topic of tuberculosis is raised in an AIDS support group, the issue of contagion accompanies it. Reactions in the group tend to be varied, running the gamut from denial, to terror in those who perceive TB as a death threat, to rage in those who perceive the agency or facilitators as not providing adequate protections against the spread of TB. Seldom is there a direct discussion of the threat of contagion among the members in the room. Although this is an area of silence in which facilitators need to offer assistance, they themselves may be in the throes of their own countertransference reactions to contagion and simply unable to press for a discussion of the threat permeating the room. This complex issue speaks to some of the more disturbed feelings of group members and facilitators alike, i.e., the threat of contagion. Molnos (1990), a British group analyst, noted that the fear of contagion associated with HIV triggers in "all of us an archaic animal fear" (p. 44). PWA groups are certainly no exception to this, and in fact such fears may be increased, bringing with them feelings of guilt and shame.

In the illustration offered here, what emerges is the complexity of the impact of a member's MDRTB on a PWA group.

Tina had AIDS for two years and joined a PWA group after she developed her second OI. She became sick again shortly after joining the group, was hospitalized and treated for TB. After being assured by her physician that she was cured, she rejoined the PWA. After a few months in the group, where she focused on issues related to the care of her children, she became sick again. This time she complained to the group of fatigue, fevers, night sweats and general malaise. She lost considerable weight and was again hospitalized. Shortly thereafter, the group learned that her TB had recurred. This time it was the multi-drug resistant strain of TB. Tina spoke to the group members by phone and related that the first time she had TB it hadn't been treated adequately and thus it had never completely re-mitted although she felt well for awhile. For Tina this meant not only many weeks away from her children and from the group, but treatment with an arsenal of drugs. For the group, the knowledge that they had been exposed week after week was never addressed. Instead the group, including the facilita-tors, continued to focus on Tina's health, recovery and return to the group. Only when the group facilitators' supervisor be-came alarmed that the facilitators and all the members had been exposed to TB were the facilitators able to discuss in their su-pervision group the pros and cons of introducing the possibility of contagion to the PWA group.

It was only with the knowledge of Tina's anticipated date of return to the group, that group members were able to talk about their fear of TB and all the thoughts and anxieties they had harbored when Tina's TB first became known.

The TB epidemic in the HIV/AIDS world has received lit-tle attention. Equally disturbing is that there has been a signif-icant increase in the exposure of health care workers to TB, and few interventions to adequately address the safety of the workplace have been made to secure it (Clever and LeGuyader, 1995).[2] This writer noted a curious phenomenon at the Gay Men's Health Crisis during the period 1990–94 after air circulating equipment was put into all the group rooms to assure that air circulated in such a way as to minimize exposure to TB bacteria. Noteworthy were the numerous reports by the group facilitators that they turned off these devices during the actual group sessions because of the noise they emitted. This behavior reportedly continued even though signs were placed on the machines indicating that they were effective only if constantly operating.

RATIONAL SUICIDE IN PWA SUPPORT GROUPS

Although there is available literature on the incidence of suicidality and suicide in persons with HIV and AIDS (Beckerman, 1995; Beltangady, 1988; Cotes, Biggar, and Dannenberg, 1992; Forstein, 1994; Frierson and Lippman, 1988; Glass, 1988; Marzuk, Tierney, Tardiff, Gross, Morgan, Hsu, and Mann, 1988; McKegney and O'Dowd, 1992; Schneider, Taylor, Kemeny, and Hammen, 1991; Werth, 1995), little has been written about the specific circumstances and clinical implications of suicidality and suicide in groups for PWAs. Rather, the focus of the writing in this area has been on right-to-die issues prompted by renewed interest in the right of the terminally ill to make decisions about their own personal dignity and quality of life, and, in the context of that to choose when and how their life will end. Such debate, captured in the actions and articulations of Dr. Jack Kevorkian[3] and in the vigorous debate over euthanasia and physician-assisted suicide (Battin, 1994; Brody, 1992; Misbin, 1991; Momeyer, 1995; Pearlman, Cain, and Patrick, 1993; Quill, 1994; Rogers and Britton, 1994; Werth, 1992), provides an important backdrop for understanding how a group member's decision to terminate life affects the group as whole, individual group members, and facilitators.

The issue of suicide when it arises in the process of a PWA group is dauntingly complex, because it frequently occurs in an atmosphere already saturated with multiple, premature loss and dominated by fear and uncertainty with regard to the future. This section deals specifically with issues related to rational suicide, or the right to die, since it appears to be one of the more frequently encountered issues in groups with PWAs. Rational suicide (Siegel, 1986; Werth, 1992) suggests that persons confronting a life course of pain, increasing disability, and physical and emotional dependence may choose, under certain circumstances, the time and method of their death. Such decisions are likened by some to the right to refuse treatment. Inherent in the concept of rational suicide is the notion that the person making a decision to end his or her life has an accurate and realistic assessment of his or her medical situation, that there exists no diagnosable, treatable psychological illness that impairs the individual's judgment and decision-making capacity, and that uninvolved others in the person's social group or community would affirm the motivation for these actions (Siegel, 1986).

More recently, Werth (1992), in a controversial article on rational suicide and AIDS, proposed a position for all therapists to assume:

> When the time comes, it will be up to each therapist to decide whether or not to be a participant in the AIDS client's search for information about and/or possible decision to commit suicide . . . Not only do I believe that a therapist should allow for the possibility of rational suicide in the case of a person with

AIDS and should not interfere in reasoned decision, I also believe that if asked, a practitioner should help such an individual explore suicide as a real and viable option. (p. 653)

Rabkin, Remien, and Wilson (1994) in their research on the relationship issues between the person with HIV and health providers suggest that there are points during the trajectory of the disease when the PWA feels enough is enough. In their observations, this is linked to "serious debilitating illness, often entailing hospitalization and usually accompanied by pain" (p. 140). The cohort of gay men in their study mentioned three conditions that would prompt them to rational suicidal ideation and actions: dementia, pain, and incontinence.

PWA support group members are all too familiar with these conditions, since they are not unusual occurrences in the course of illness for some members. In many instances, the illness often necessitates the member leaving the group or having phone sessions or visits by the group in the home or hospital room. In these instances the group members may become not only witnesses to but participants in a process whereby a member has moved from a stance of active hope of a cure in the time remaining to questions about terminating life. Some members may identify with the dying member's questions and thoughts about terminating life, while others may not identify, believing instead that the member is choosing death, not that death is the inevitable result of the illness. Such a situation has a powerful and complex influence on the future of the group's dynamics. It may constitute an event that unifies the group, promoting further empowerment and connection. Or it may create fragmentation within the group, whereby members abandon the group, viewing it now not as a healing, hopeful context but as a disabling and even malignant force. Rational suicide is a powerful issue and force in all groups for people with AIDS and must be reckoned with, openly and actively. Beckett and Rutan (1990), reflecting on their two-year experience with four AIDS groups, observed:

> The issue of suicide weaves in and out of these groups. Suicide in this context has multiple and subtle meanings. It is at times the answer to the question of how one may have control where control is fragmentary at best. It may offer a solution to the dilemma of what to do with life when it becomes truly unbearable. It may herald the loss of hope accompanying yet another opportunistic infection, a new Kaposi's sarcoma lesion, neurological symptoms such as memory loss and paralysis, inexorable weight loss, or abandonment by significant persons. The therapist must learn to listen to suicidal ideation as both a metaphor and potential reality. (p. 23)

Given the nature and unpredictable course of AIDS illness as well as the controversial, complicated issue of rational suicide that often arises in PWA support groups, group facilitators are frequently confronted with difficult therapeutic and ethical dilemmas in the life and processes of their support groups. Few writers in the area of group work with persons with AIDS articulate or elaborate on the dynamics of group process when rational suicidal ideation or action occurs within the group (Beckett and Rutan, 1990; Frost, 1992; Field and Shore, 1992). The dearth of literature may reflect the ethical dilemmas, countertransference reactions, and general uneasiness practitioners experience in exploring and discussing these issues in professional settings or professional journals.

Professional literature on suicide in groups, although meager (Buelow, 1994; Kibel, 1973; Kirtley, 1969), point to the fact that most suicides are understood not as rational acts but instead as a sudden, unpredictable acting out of destructive impulses. Anecdotal reports on groups where such events have occurred suggest that members often responded to even rational suicides with considerable denial and disbelief. In one group, members reflected on how awareness that a member was considering death as an option in the face of illness did little to diminish their disbelief that the person had actually ended his life.

S. was a member of a support group for two years. During the six months subsequent to leaving his job and developing CMV he started talking of his plan to end his life should his situation worsen. S. remained in the group, talking intermittently about this issue of suicide. S. was also in individual treatment, a factor which seemed to relieve many of the group members who at times had trouble managing their feelings about S.'s situation. S.'s situation did worsen and within a year he was too ill to participate regularly in the group. Five weeks after last seeing S., the group learned of his suicide from the facilitators who were notified by his family. The following are the responses of some of the group members on the evening of the announcement: "I know it but I still don't believe it."

"Me, too, he was so strong in the beginning. He really believed he would be one of the long term survivors. I believed it too. I think he did a good job of it. Do we know how he did it?"

"I heard he used the *Final Exit* method—pills and a plastic bag. I still do not believe it!"

"I wish he had told us more about the details. I do not know why, I just wish I knew more."

"Me, I'm going to do the exact same thing. Can't take the blindness, just like S. I wouldn't be able to take it either."

"I think he would have lasted if he hadn't lost so much weight. He said, he was so fatigued that holding his head up was a big deal."

Anecdotal reporting of rational suicides in groups with PWAs suggests that facilitators should be prepared to initiate or encourage frank discussion of the suicide of a member and the range of feelings and viewpoints associated with the event, emphasizing the effect of the member's suicide on each of them as well as their feelings about the group, given this event. It is noteworthy that members have often "forgotten" the details of the member's planned death. This may signal that although it was planned, the suicide was for the surviving members a traumatic event that demands more attention, discussion, and working through. The denial of death is an ever-present mechanism in these groups, and its tenacity is often illustrated by the shock response to a planned death.

If rational suicides do occur and group members and facilitators are aware of them, it becomes crucial to understand their effect on the group process. What happens to a group when one of its members, after months of deterioration and pain related to AIDS, completes a plan to take his or her life? How is it processed by the remaining group members? And how do facilitators negotiate their feelings as well as their role, given the history of such an event in the group's life?

These are but some of the pressing emotional and psychological questions permeating and propelling the group dynamics following the rational suicide of a group member. The responses may be similar to those of all suicide survivors, and the group, its members, and the facilitator may struggle with the reactions identified by Farberow (1992) in his summary of the experiences of suicide survivors in an after-suicide program. These experiences included strong feelings of loss accompanied by sorrow and mourning; anger at being made to feel responsible; feelings of separation because the help offered was refused; anxiety, guilt, shame, or embarrassment; relief that nagging, insistent demands have ceased; feelings of having been deserted; arousal of one's impulses toward suicide and anger caused by the belief that the suicide represents a rejection of social and moral responsibilities (in Valente 1994).

MULTIPLE DEATHS AS A SPECIAL ISSUE IN PWA SUPPORT GROUPS

The death of group members, whether suddenly or expectedly, is a common demoninator of many ongoing AIDS support groups. It requires ongoing attention and consideration by both group members and facilitators. However, the consequences of these deaths are conceptualized—as massive bereavement (Blechner, 1993), multiple loss syndrome (Cheh and Cassidy, 1994), repeated bereavement (Kemeny, Weiner, Taylor, Schneider, Visscher, and Fahey, 1994), multiple death survivors (Gabriel, 1991), repeated survivors (Goldman, 1989), bereavement overload (Dane, 1994; Hirsch and Enlow, 1984; Strawn, 1987), bereavement epidemic (Lennon, Martin, and Dean, 1990), or chronic bereavement (Rando,

1984)—they relegate death to the "here-and-now," producing a phenomenon akin to posttraumatic stress in families (Brende and Goldsmith, 1991). These authors suggest that traumata, especially suicide, homicide, sudden violent deaths, or witnessing family violence, sexual abuse, and assaults may precipitate a family victimization cycle that requires intervention to prevent what these authors refer to as a "family death." Such a cycle is characterized by traumatic event, followed by states of a family member's alienation and isolation, shame, fragmentation, and secrets, and eventuates in the family's disintegration. Such a cycle may develop as well in a group where bereavement has constituted a major group activity and where chronic bereavement has been relentless.

Such bereavement in these groups is rooted in a reality that makes the bereavement process itself complex. Specifically, the expectable reality of AIDS involves death and grieving among those in early and middle adulthood; those who are left to grieve are frequently diagnosed with HIV themselves; the confrontation of frequent sequential losses disrupts the normal processes of grieving so that the grieving processes are never completed (Martin, 1988).

The only literature to date on the impact of multiple deaths of persons with AIDS comes from the examination of the experience of gay men in bereavement. Commenting on the consequences of AIDS bereavement, the investigators Lennon, Martin, and Dean (1990) note:

the AIDS epidemic is producing a situation in which grieving may become an unrelenting process with little opportunity for recovery. This is particularly true for individuals such as gay men, whose network consists primarily of individuals at risk for

AIDS. Recovering from grief will be hampered not only by multiple losses close in time but also by the loss to illness and death of the very people previously relied on for help and comfort. Given these conditions support for those close to and for those who care for persons with AIDS is essential. (p. 483)

These authors identified a casual relationship between bereavement episodes and the experience of traumatic stress response symptoms in a cohort of gay men, reinforcing the notion of the trauma of witnessing and grieving multiple deaths.

The literature on AIDS and AIDS bereavement speaks to the issue of survivor's guilt as a major phenomenon associated with the multiple-death phenomenon and the massive bereavement experience confronting the PWA (Amelio, 1993; Boykin, 1991; Doka, 1987; Houseman and Pheifer, 1988; Odets, 1994; Oerleman-Bunn, 1988; Schwartzberg, 1992). Those who witness become "survivors," and according to Lifton (1982) there is a definite psychology to survivorship. Lifton defines a survivor as "one who comes into contact with death in some bodily or psychic fashion and has remained alive" (p. 1014). Such a definition may be applied to members and facilitators of support groups for PWAs who have witnessed the deaths of other members while confronting their own. Lifton's observations on survivorship and on reactions to multiple trauma have lead to the emergence of five themes drawn from the narratives of survivors: the death imprint, death guilt, psychic numbing, conflict around nurturing and contagion, and struggles with life meaning. Each of these themes emerges in these groups, especially as the group encounters the deaths of more members and attempts to mourn and make meaning of each loss. Not only is the membership mourned but eventually the group's original membership may be deceased or absent. Ultimately the facilitators and a few members may be left to mourn that first group.

For Lifton, survivor's guilt represents a conflict between mourning the lost object while simultaneously feeling relief that one has survived. The existential question for the survivor then becomes, Why did I survive while they died? The answer becomes yet another question: Did I survive while letting them die? As Lifton (1982) states:

> One could define the traumatic syndrome [survivor's guilt] as the state of being haunted by images that can neither be enacted nor cast aside. Suffering is associated with being "stuck". Hence the indelible image is always associated with guilt and in its most intense form takes the shape of an image of ultimate horror: a single image (often containing brutalized children or dying people whom the survivor often loved) . . . Only part of oneself feels discomfort at having survived—the experience is also associated with relief, even joy or exhilaration. These feelings can, in turn, contribute to additional guilt. (p. 1016)

Manifestations of Survivor's Guilt in Support Groups for PWAs

Essentially the manifestations of some aspect of survivor's guilt are evidenced in the communication between group members. Usually occurring after a death, these discussions and revelations take the form of questioning the randomness of the illness and its unpredictable course. At these times it becomes clear to the listener that the experience of multiple deaths in these groups parallels the members' experience outside the groups and in the community at large.

Here I have been losing weight for months. And shitting my brains out every day and he dies. Explain that. He dies, Bill dies, Hank dies, Leo dies. They all die! Why haven't I died? I should have died a long time ago. How many years do you have to live with this scourge? Is there a purpose to watching all my friends die? Have I been spared or have I been cursed?

After a series of three deaths in this group over a period of eight months the group's survival becomes an issue. Here survivor's guilt may encompass the group as a totality. A member, Michael, addresses this possibility in response to the death of Robert, the most recent member of the group to die. Michael had grown very attached to Robert, and although they did not live together and each has a care partner, they were essentially "buddies" in AIDS.

"I don't think it's AIDS that killed Robert. I think it is this group. There has to be a reason why he was doing so well and then he dies. I am telling you, it's this group!" The facilitators, in response, inquired as to whether or not the group was interested in hearing Michael's theory about the "group killing." Group members excitedly begin talking: "Yeah, yeah, it's a killing alright. He is dead, B. is dead and H., he is dead too. How come them, because they have been here the longest? In fact, I've been here the longest and I am next. I can't understand why Robert died. I mean, he wasn't that sick. You saw him. He was the same old Robert. It wasn't his turn. It was my turn. Aren't we taking turns? Isn't that what this seems to be, a group waiting to die?

Here elements of the toxicity of death are mingled with the survivor's guilt experienced by Michael, who not only lost an important connection but also was unable to confront the fact that he was still living while Robert, who was less visibly ill, had died. Such attempts to make meaning as well as deny any relief at being spared highlight the group processes after such a series of deaths, or sudden death. The fact that these groups are for people with AIDS, that each member has been treated for opportunistic infections, that many are visibly ill, that there are numerous conversations about death, that death has been a part of each of their experiences in this last decade does not diminish the enormous denial whenever death enters these groups. This collective lot of significant figures and symbols of support and connection traumatizes the survivors and creates an impact that is at first essentially denied. Only through partializing and identification with those who are able to speak directly to these events are these groups able to move toward some semblance of mourning. As one person with AIDS confided to investigators in a study of long-term survivors of HIV (Remien and Wagner, 1994):

> There is a sense of constant loss. And the longer you live with this thing, the more losses there are. There never seems to be a reward for being a long-term survivor. It's just long grief. (p. 184)

SUMMARY

The five special considerations and issues discussed in this chapter represent but a few of the issues that contribute to the complexity of AIDS support groups. Obviously, other special circumstances need to be addressed, such as the impact of deterioration of members on other group members and facilitators, the management of outside group contacts for members and facilitators, the merging of groups, issues of self-disclosure by facilitators of their own HIV/AIDS status, the impact of a facilitator death on such groups, and a host of other topics. The issues discussed here were considered to be the most frequently cited in the current literature and the most frequently reported upon in AIDS supervision groups. Of these five issues—confidentiality, dementia, tuberculosis, rational suicide, and multiple deaths—the most troublesome and as yet unstudied in terms of group theory is the effects of multiple deaths and massive bereavement on group processes. Obviously this epidemic has created substantial need for creative review and reenvisioning of both our therapeutic understanding and interventions. What happens to an individual's or group's capacity to mourn when the mourning involves whole families, communities, and support networks, and when the mourners are themselves confronting the prospect of untimely illness and death? There is no doubt that one major therapeutic force in attempting to ameliorate the impact of such trauma is group intervention.

CHAPTER 4

Countertransference Reactions in Facilitators of PWA Support Groups

Death Anxiety, Contagion Anxiety, Identification, Helplessness, Envy, Anger, and Rage

The publication of David W. Winnicott's (1947) paper on objective countertransference, coupled with the observations on the subject by Heimann (1950), Little (1951), Racker (1953, 1957), and Kernberg (1964), posed a challenge to the prevailing view of countertransference as a hindrance to the therapeutic endeavor. Their observations lead to a conceptualization of countertransference as a phenomenon that enhances the therapeutic communication processes in both individual and group practice, leading to greater understanding among therapist and patient, client, group member(s), or the group as a whole. Explorations of countertransference reactions have extended beyond the parameters of psychoanalytic practices to general clinical literature of all mental health and health professions. The advent of traumatology has generated renewed interest in the concept of countertransference, as seen in professional literature during the last fifteen years. Recent interest (Wilson and Lindy, 1995) has focused on understanding therapists' countertransference reactions in the context of therapeutic work with Holocaust survivors (Danielli, 1984), Vietnam veterans (Lindy, 1988), rape survivors (Hartman and Jackson, 1994), domestic abuse survivors (Herman, 1992), survivors of physical and sexual abuse (Shay, 1992), incest survivors (McElroy and McElroy, 1991; Pearlman and Saakvitne, 1995), survivors of catastrophic injury (Gunter, 1994), survivors of natural disaster (Karakashian, 1994), survivors of massive violence (Kinzie and Boehnlein, 1993), and persons with AIDS (Dunkel and Hatfield, 1988; Macks, 1988). This chapter discusses the role of countertransference in therapeutic work and its particular manifestations in AIDS-related therapeutic work and in group therapies, including AIDS support groups.

THE CONCEPTS: COUNTERTRANSFERENCE

In contrast to the concept of transference, countertransference was not systematically explored by Freud. With its introduction into the psychoanalytic literature (Freud, 1910), Freud described it as arising in the practitioner "as a result of the patient's influence on his unconscious." It was defined as those feelings and thoughts produced by the analyst during time with a patient. It was considered a hindrance to the therapeutic process, arising from the analyst's past and suggestive of unresolved issues. Freud admonished therapists to "recognize this . . . and overcome it." From 1910 until the publications of Winnicott, Heinman, and Racker in the late

1940s and early 1950s, countertransference was viewed as an obstacle to therapeutic progress and something the therapist must strive to "get over."

Since the 1950s, however, the concept has been reconceptualized and expanded to include all the feelings, thoughts, affects, and fantasies of the therapist about the patient, client, or group members or group during the course of the treatment relationship. The generally accepted definition was offered by Paula Heimann (1950):

> I am using the term "countertransference" to cover all the feelings which the analyst experiences toward his patient . . . My thesis is that the analyst's emotional response to his patient within the analytic situation represents one of the most important tools for his work. The analyst's countertransference is an instrument of research into the patient's unconscious. (p. 81)

Heimann, disagreeing with the view of countertransference as a negative phenomenon, turned her attention to its potential value in furthering therapeutic work. This view, coupled with Winnicott's observations on "truly objective countertransference" (Winnicott, 1949), highlighted the necessity of the analyst's examining, tolerating, and understanding the feelings of love and hate toward a patient, because these reactions to the personality and behavior of the patient may be based on objective reality. With these changed and expanded notions, countertransference became recognized as an important avenue for understanding the diagnosis and the communications made by patients. What was essential to this understanding was that the analyst had a full range of feelings that could be used toward understanding the patient/client. Abandoned was the notion that an analyst was supposed to harbor only mild benevolence toward patients and that any ripple of emotion on this smooth surface represented a disturbance to be overcome.

Racker (1953, 1957) and Kernberg (1964) elaborated on the concept of countertransference by introducing topology to the phenomenon. Racker described two types of countertransferences, which may be utilized to determine inner emotional constellations of the patient: "concordant identifications" and "commentary identification." In the concordant identification, one part of the therapist's psychic apparatus identifies with the corresponding part of the patient's psychic apparatus, e.g., ego with ego, superego with superego. As a consequence the therapist may experience the central emotion that the patient is experiencing at the same time. Thus empathy might be considered in Racker's classification a direct expression of a concordant identification. Complementary identification, elaborated upon by Racker as a second type, refers to the identification of the therapist with the transference objects of the patient. In this position the therapist is experiencing the emotion the patient is experiencing about past interactions with particular parental images. In Racker's conceptualization the therapist fluctuates between these two kinds of countertransference identifications.

Kernberg, in his writing on this topic in 1964, distinguished between the classical approach and the totalistic approach to countertransference. While the classical approach conceptualized countertransference reactions as rising from unresolved neurotic conflicts of the therapist, the totalistic approach views countertransference as the total emotional reaction of the therapist to the patient in the treatment situation. This totalistic view, represented by the writings of Racker and

Winnicott, reflects the belief that with highly regressed patients the countertransference becomes an important diagnostic and treatment tool. Kernberg suggests that such countertransference "duplicates the experience of the patient" and that the analyst may not always "snap out" of the countertransference inducement. Instead, certain patients may precipitate a "fixed" countertransference position, resulting in distorted interactions between patient and analyst.

Spotnitz (1987) made reference to two types of countertransference: subjective and objective. The subjective is based on the therapist's own adjustment patterns, i.e., feelings that the therapist developed from significant figures in his or her own life, often reawakened by the patient's transference. Of the objective type, Spotnitz believed this type of countertransference referred to emotions that are realistically induced (Winnicott, 1949) in the therapist and can be utilized in various ways to benefit the patient.

McDougall (1979), writing more recently on countertransference, introduces yet another type of reaction. She observed that in patients with preverbal traumas there was "fundamental transference" and primitive communications:

> The patients who I have in mind use speech in a way that has little in common with the language of free association. In listening to them the analyst may have a feeling that it is a meaningless communication at all levels, or he may be aware of being invaded with affect which does not seem directly attributable to the content of the patient's communication. The question is how to understand and use such countertransference affect. I hope to show in this article that these analysands frequently use language as an *act* rather than a symbolic means of communica-

tion of ideas or affect. At such times, unknown to analyst and patient alike, the latter is revealing the effect of a catastrophic failure in communication which has occurred at a time when he was unable to contain or to work through, psychically, what he was experiencing. (p. 272)

Observations on this concept come from analysts who were concerned with therapeutic work with those with compromised, regressed, or rather primitive self and ego states. Thus for these theorists, conscious communication vis-à-vis "induced feeling states" became essential to understanding of experiences that these patients were unable to communicate in language. A parallel may be drawn from the study of "induced feeling states" in work with highly regressed patients to work with persons surviving trauma whose egos have, temporarily at least, been overwhelmed with affect resulting in muted, numbing, detached states often characterized by frequent lapses into silence. For this group as well, induced feelings, as objective countertransference reactions, may communicate states of feeling that are momentarily unavailable in language.

Countertransference Reactions in Group Therapies

In group therapies the concepts of transference and countertransference are defined similarly, accommodating to the presence and impact of multiple persons. Such a therapeutic situation constitutes what Slavson (1950) referred to as a "network of transferences." Thus there are multiple transferences to the leader, lateral (member-to-member) transferences, and group-as-a-whole transferences. Similarly, the therapist's countertransference reactions, subjective and objective and multiple, include therapist to therapist (cotherapy), therapist to individual members, therapist to subgroup of members, and therapist to the group as a whole. A major task for the group practitioner is to promote interaction among group members and help individual members become a part of the group, while at the same time attending to the impact of each member's particular character style and reaction on others and on the process of interacting. There is no doubt that this task, coupled with the group atmosphere, exposes the group practitioner to high doses of affect and information from the group as a whole as well as from individual members. In this setting a host of countertransference reactions, both subjective and objective, emerges. Similar to reactions that emerge in individual practice, these countertransference reactions are specific to a given group and a given group life. However, the literature suggests that there are some general subjective and objective countertransference reactions of group practitioners that are noteworthy and thus important enough to enumerate and elaborate upon here.

Subjective Countertransference Reaction in Group Practice

Mullan (1970) observed that the group situation brings forth and sharply delineates dormant subjective countertransference reactions in much greater number and intensity than may occur in individual therapy. One such countertransference reaction noted by Flapan and Fenchel (1984) is a "stereotyped role" of the group practitioner who focuses exclusively on one individual member or on the group. The authors suggest:

Those who focus on the group and neglect the individual in the group may be afraid that by focusing on the individual they will encounter group anger . . . Others may feel insecure and ill-equipped to be able to give to both the individuals and the group at the same time and so choose to concentrate on the group. These therapists may cling to the fantasy that the group will do the therapeutic work and that in this way they can avoid exposing their own shortcomings as group therapists. The therapist may then promote a narcissistic overvaluation of "the group" and its "curative" elements at the expense of individual members. (pp. 22 & 23)

Other reactions that may relate to the group practitioner's own issues and constitute a subjective countertransference reaction are allying with the group against one member; conducting individual treatment in group, overinterpreting, over-explaining, overadvising without consulting group members, who are in most instances well acquainted with the content or interaction under examination; poorly tolerating or not tolerating silences, believing them to have only one meaning, or else tolerating too much silence (Flapan and Fenchel, 1984). Slavson (1953), a major group theorist and prolific writer in this area, suggested that the source of all subjective countertransference for the therapist as well as the group members lay within their families of origin.

Anxiety in human groups also stems from earlier family relations. Attitudes and responses toward groups are replicas of family experiences. Every group, particularly small groups, represent in the unconscious of the individual his family, and he inevitably acts out the primary relations in them. (p. 386)

Slavson, joined by Solomon, Loeffler, and Frank (1953), Hadden (1953), and Frank (1953), discussed the types of subjective countertransference experienced by group psychotherapists. Slavson identified and provided examples of positive, negative, and therapeutic ambition (aim attachment) subjective countertransference responses. In the negative subjective state, which he believed to be of more frequent occurrence than any other countertransference states in group etiology, was the group practitioner's own family of origin.

> The painful memories aroused in the therapist by a variety of patient are always likely to activate in him either conscious or unconscious feelings of discomfort, fear of hostility or anger in relation to one or more persons in a group. Some may resemble parents, siblings, teachers or others who had hurt or injured him or had in some other way made him feel unhappy in childhood. (p. 376)

Positive subjective countertransference may arise from the therapist's need to be liked by patients, thereby manifesting preference for the group members who show or convey overt pleasure at or approval of the therapist's therapeutic activity. The third subjective countertransference reaction discussed by these authors and first mentioned by Slavson is aim attachment; this refers to the therapist's internal and external need for success, a need that may inspire the therapist's interventions regardless of the needs of the group.

> Our need to succeed is not a part of our relations to the patient. Nor is it tied up with the patient himself. Rather frequently it is necessary for us, for our own personal survival, to see that our patients improve. . . . These external needs for success are one

of the greatest sources of what we have been discussing here, namely aim attachment countertransference.... Hence the therapist who fails in improving the patient cannot but suspect his own inadequacy as being the cause. (p. 381)

Solomon, Loeffler, and Frank (1953) identified a fourth type of subjective countertransference based on their examination of the experiences of cotherapists. This fourth type they termed ambivalent and inconsistent countertransference reaction, arising from the nature of relationships/interactions between cotherapists. Cotherapists may be inconsistent in their responses to the group and group members as a result of some unresolved differences in their cotherapy relationship.

Ormont (1992a) identified and discussed four different kinds of subjective countertransference that may occur in a group therapy setting. He refers to these as subjective ego, id, superego, and secondary gain. In the subjective ego countertransference, the group leader is believed to find some feeling state unacceptable because of an unresolved early life experience and therefore interrupts its expression in the group. In the id form of subjective countertransference, the group leader abandons the role of leader to obtain some form of instinctual gratification. A case in point would be a situation in which the leader initiates some activity among group members without exploration of its meaning to the group and its members. The superego countertransference reaction occurs when the leader is provoked by members to act in an unacceptable manner resulting in the therapist's guilt and shame. Secondary gain countertransference is operative when the group leader finds unexpected personal gain and pleasure from the group experience that is outside the boundaries of satisfaction from the work but rather related to certain behaviors in the group that are continued because they provide the leader pleasure. Ormont gives the example of a talk group that gradually becomes a music group playing music each week instead of addressing the contracted task of talking.

Rosenthal (1987), writing on the subject of group resistances and their resolution, makes reference to subjective countertransference phenomena in group by describing constellations of feelings that the group practitioner may bring from earlier life experiences to the group experience, further elaborating on Slavson's types of subjective countertransference reactions. These include the need for a happy family, the need to be liked and reactions to aggression and hostility, reactions to competition and opposition, therapeutic zeal, and identification with group members. Each of these fuels a certain subjective response in the leader. For example, Rosenthal suggests that the need for a happy family may influence the therapist's interventions to suppress feelings of resentment, rivalry, hostility, and anger. The need to be liked may lead the group practitioner to avoid aggression, counterattack, and other behaviors expressive of anger or discontent. Subjective countertransference reactions to competition and opposition may prompt a group leader to engage in overdetermined assertions of authority or control. And therapeutic zeal may prompt a group practitioner to make unrealistic demands on group members and the group with regard to their functioning. In identifying with group members, the group leader appears to abandon the role of active listener, thereby losing the capacity to make use of the various group members' interactions.

Identification As a Subjective Countertransference Reaction

Loeser and Bry (1953) studied countertransference phenomena in group therapists and identified several sources. For them the most common and most powerful sources of these reactions were based on the therapist's "concordant and complementary identifications" with the members in the group (Racker, 1953).

> By this we mean identification with the patient with the patient's problem of the moment and material being produced or with symptoms and similar processes. When identification on the part of the therapist occurs in an area in which his own psychodynamic processes are in conflict, anxiety or tension arises or it leads to acting out . . . On the other hand, identification, well integrated and capable of interpretation, provides the therapist with an awareness and sensitivity which is invaluable and is probably a necessary aspect of therapy. (p. 394)

Commenting on the resistance aspect of identification, Rosenthal (1987) observes that in these instances of identification, the therapist is unable to separate emotionally from the patient with whom he or she identifies. In this instance the therapist is not able to "snap out of" (Kernberg, 1964) the countertransference, as it were, and therefore is not liberated to use his or her own induced feelings and reactions to the patient because they are the same as the patient's. For example, if a group member with whom the group practitioner identifies complains of not being helped or understood by the group leader or by the group, the therapist may assume the member's complaints are justified, thereby avoiding or truncating any further exploration or expression of the member's distress. Thus, the subjective experience of the therapist thwarts the therapist from utilizing fully all avenues of communication.

Objective Countertransference Reactions in Group Practice

Martin Grotjahn (1953), writing when group theorists were struggling to integrate observations on countertransference with group dynamics and processes, suggested that objective countertransference was essential to the group practitioner's understanding of the group members:

> As the group progresses to a working unit, multiple transference relationships will be developed and the therapist will react with feelings of countertransference. He needs this feeling in order to establish contact and to understand by empathy his patients' transferences. (p. 410)

Objective countertransference leading to induced feelings, as discussed above, emerges as unconscious messages are sent by the group to the therapist. As Spotnitz (1968) states:

> Constant exposure to the instinctual forces operating simultaneously in the group members generates strong feelings in the therapist. If these are conceptualized as countertransference, they should be differentiated from feeling responses related to his own adjustment patterns. The feelings that are induced by the members' transference emotions are realistic reactions to what is going on in the group. (p. 21)

Ormont, writing in 1970, illustrated the manner by which the group practitioner may use these induced feelings to facilitate group interventions. He suggested that objective countertransference feelings are a natural product of group interactions.

> They are vital, if primitive, messages he is receiving from the members' shared unconscious emotions. These messages may greatly aid him in reconstructing the meaningful shared history of his group members. Reactions induced in him can serve as a key with which he can unlock the imprisoned aspect in the group member. In addition, his reactions can also serve as a beacon to him, guiding him back to the therapeutic path from which the group shared obstacles may have diverted him. (p. 96)

His approach to the use of objective countertransference reactions relied heavily on the group practitioner's study of his or her own responses. Such restraining of actions facilitates the identification of the meaning these feeling states have for the group. He provides several examples of how some practitioners avoid these induced feelings and choose instead to view them as subjective countertransference reactions, i.e., as reactions to be resolved and banished through self-enlightenment or as incentives to plunge into some kind of action. In discouraging both these approaches, Ormont cautions that the use of induced feelings involves recognition of certain principles of group practice, namely, examination of the group practitioner's resistance to experiencing these feelings as induced by the group; development of a working tolerance for the feelings; temporarily identifying with them, then returning to a more objective stance of studying the various motives and attitudes that may underlie this inducement; and working at diminishing the defenses surrounding the direct expression of these feelings in words.

Yalom in his classic text on group psychotherapy, first written in 1970 and in a recent fourth edition (1995), advanced an interpersonal model of group psychotherapy focusing on character change and insight through the group's work in the here and now. Writing within this framework, he makes reference to the power of subjective countertransference reactions:

> The therapist's self-knowledge plays a role in every aspect of therapy. An inability to perceive countertransference responses, to recognize personal distortions and blind spots, or to use one's own feelings and fantasies in one's work will limit the effectiveness of any therapists. If you lack insight into your own motivations, for example, you may avoid conflict in the group because of your proclivity to mute your feelings; or you may unduly encourage confrontation in a search for aliveness in yourself. You may be overeager to prove yourself or to make consistently brilliant interpretations, and thereby emasculate the group. You may fear intimacy and prevent open expression of feelings by premature interpretations—or do the opposite: overemphasize feelings, make too few connections, and overstimulate patients so that they are left in agitated turmoil. You may so need acceptance that you are unable to challenge the group and, like the members, may be swept along by the prevailing group current. You may be so devastated by an attack on yourself and so unclear about your presentation of self as to be unable to distinguish the realistic from the transference aspects of the attack. (pp. 526–27)

In elucidating the processes of working in the here and now with a group, Yalom acknowledges the importance of the "therapist's feelings." His observations suggest he is speaking of induced feelings and objective countertransference.

All of these guides to the therapist's recognition and understanding of process have their usefulness. But there is an even
more important clue: The therapist's own feelings in the meeting, feelings that he or she has come to trust after living
through many previous similar incidents in group therapy. Experienced therapists learn to trust their feelings; they are as
useful to a therapist as a microscope to a microbiologist. If
therapists feel impatient, frustrated, bored, confused, discouraged—any of the entire panoply of feelings available to a
human being—they consider this valuable data and learn to
put it to work. (p. 159)

In this latter paragraph, Yalom reflects thinking similar to
that of Margaret Little, some forty-five years ago, when she
advanced the notion that analysts should share with patients
certain aspects of the objective countertransference reactions.
Yalom, in the vein of Little, Ormont, and others who have
spoken of using objective countertransference, cautions therapists that such use must grow out of the therapist's self-
enlightenment. Without such enlightenment, use of the therapist's feelings may lead to misuse of the group and perhaps
even narcissistic injury to its members.

COUNTERTRANSFERENCE REACTIONS IN WORK
WITH THE MEDICALLY ILL

Using Winnicott's observations on objective countertransference, Alder (1984) discusses some of the problems encountered by therapists in the treatment of the medically ill patient.
He conceptualizes the dynamics between some therapists and
patients as projective identification. First a patient may project

anger and hate toward the therapist based on feelings about being treated by someone who is thought to be medically well. The therapist responds with feelings of hate toward the patient. He observed:

> For some of these patients the provoked hate confirms their expectations that their illness, deterioration and impending death is unbearable to professionals who should be capable of tolerating it. These projective identification issues compound the hate problems the treaters already have in working with the physically ill. (pp. 94–95)

Adler suggests that this countertransference hate of the medically ill patient may be used creatively. The therapists' self-acknowledgment and owning of their hate for the patient may signal identification with the patient's current state and in some instances facilitate the patient in confronting his or her hate for the therapist and other caregivers for their perceived "wellness."

Norton (1963), writing on her experience of working psychoanalytically with a dying patient, cogently offers her understanding of the function of hate directed toward her by the patient:

> Discussion of the irritation brought into focus her intense envy of me which had been present and unverbalized from the beginning. She envied my relative youth, my health, my activity, the fact I was not sick and helpless as she was. (p. 551)

A major work in the area of countertransference reactions to medically ill patients is reflected in a classic article by Renneker (1957). This was one of the first psychoanalytic investigations to focus on the countertransference reactions in a group of seven psychoanalysts analyzing their work with women with breast cancer. In this project, Renneker and his associates identified three particular countertransference reactions: the undermining of omnipotence, the threat of narcissistic injury, and the threat to therapeutic hope. As he noted:

> When your patient developed a reoccurrence or a metastasis, your dream was shattered. It meant that you had failed somehow as a therapist. We tended within the group to substantiate this by silently blaming the analyst. (p. 413)

With regard to identification, Renneker found that the analysts resisted empathizing with patients, i.e., they resisted putting themselves in the position of the dying person, instead reporting wishes that the patient would "hurry up and die." He speculated that this death wish toward the patient arose out of the discomfort of the therapist and was a countertransference response that assisted each therapist in remaining at an emotional distance.

Countertransference Reactions in Work with PWAs

In reviewing the literature on countertransference reactions in work with PWAs, we note that the majority of observations are drawn from therapeutic work with individuals (Cadwell, 1994b; Dunkel and Hatfield, 1986; McKusick, 1988; Macks, 1988; and Namir and Sherman, 1989). Only recently have group practitioners begun to document their observations of this phenomenon (Beckett and Rutan, 1990; Bernstein and Klein, 1995; Field and Shore, 1992; Frost, 1993; Gabriel,

1991; Molnos, 1990; Tunnell, 1991). Taken collectively, these authors suggest a range of countertransference reactions viewed as subjective countertransference that pertains to the therapist's/facilitator's own internal processes. The reactions most frequently cited include death anxiety; fear of contagion; experience of helplessness; survivor's guilt; fixed or overidentification; envy, anger, and projective identification; and a range of negative reactions to the person with the disease, i.e., homophobia, racism, sexism, and addictophobia. Macks (1988) speaks to the sexism and identifies those reactions emerging in work with women with HIV/AIDS. These responses fall into the subjective countertransference category and include victim blaming and biases around a woman's decision to continue her pregnancy, become pregnant, avoid telling her diagnosis, or planning for children in the face of deteriorating health. Cadwell (1994b) focuses on the specific issues of overidentification as a countertransference reaction in gay male therapists to PWAs.

Namir and Sherman (1989) relate their subjective countertransferential reactions to the new roles that the HIV/AIDS therapist must assume when doing AIDS-related work. Among these they cite the role of hospital or home visitor, medical information specialist, and advocate with family, friends, and medical team. These "new roles" are sometimes assumed unknowingly by therapists who have not thought through what psychotherapy with a PWA may involve. This may contribute to a host of countertransference reactions that emanate from the therapist's own responses to these roles.

Sadowy (1991) reflected on the question of her role as a psychotherapist to a women, Dee, dying of AIDS on the occasion of a hospital visit to this patient.

I was immediately reminded of AIDS by the two large red bags that were placed just outside her doorway. These red bags were used for everything she uses: linens, paper dishes, tissue—everything. My anxiety heightened as I thought, "What am I doing here? Who am I to this woman?" This was neither a family member nor a more anonymous patient I had been assigned to care for as a member of the hospital staff. Our relationship was unique and had its own feelings and expectations. Above Dee's bed was a sign, not big but a warning: Infectious Disease: Precaution To Be Taken When Dealing with Bodily Fluids, Wash Hands, Wear Gloves. Here it was again: AIDS. Something felt new and threatening. Here was once a vital and verbal woman who could now not move or speak. Verbal communication, our expertise, was useless. (p. 203)

Death Anxiety, Identification, and Helplessness

Death anxiety regarding the experience of dying and the state of death provides the source of one of the major countertransference reactions in work with PWAs. This anxiety relates to any or all of the following: fearing extinction, fearing the personal suffering and physical alterations brought about by dying and death, fearing the indignity of the dying process, and fearing punishment and rejection in an afterlife (Kastenbaum and Aisenberg, 1972; Lonetto and Templer, 1986).

As Namir and Sherman (1989) observed:

Perhaps the most salient issue that therapists working with persons with AIDS must confront is their own mortality. Most individuals do not confront the inevitability of their own death, but rather operate under a system of denial and invulnerability. However, when one works with persons with AIDS, and especially those clients who are near death, it is impossible to maintain one's sense of invulnerability, or to continue to deny the potential of one's own loss and the anxieties that losses often generate. (p. 268)

Realization of the finality of one's life may precipitate for some therapists an existential crisis. From an existential viewpoint, the absolute limit imposed by death on existence generates considerable "dread" of not being. As a consequence, much human activity is organized around the drive to keep awareness of our own death out of consciousness (Becker, 1973). From this dread of death may emerge a series of subjective countertransference reactions including reexamination of one's own beliefs about illness, death, and dying and reactions to witnessing illness and death. Eissler (1955) reflected in one of the first books on the psychology of the dying patient that therapists to the dying must anticipate partial identification with the patient, joining the patient by imaging his or her own death. Such partial identifications may be understood as objective countertransference reactions and may, as he suggested, ameliorate the patient's loneliness. However, this has a subjective component as well and may evoke in therapists enormous death anxiety, which they may primitively strive to repress to avoid feelings of helplessness stimulated by confrontation with their own death. At these moments the therapist may assume the countertransference position of denial, reassurance, false optimism, or intellectualization, thereby putting out of mind any further thinking about his or her own death. The intensity of this "confrontation" with one's own mortality in AIDS work may be attributed to several factors. The most significant is perhaps that those afflicted are mostly young. Men and women in the third or fourth decade of life are generally viewed as productive and vigorous. In our society, deterioration and death on this scale in this age group has occurred only during war and is something grossly untimely and out of context. And the actual physical confrontation by helping professionals of the devastation wrought by the disease suggests images of the Holocaust. These two factors taken collectively may prompt a death imprint (Lifton, 1979) of a traumatic nature in those working with PWAs.

Yalom (1980) identifies two modes of death denial. One consists of the belief in one's own specialness, which will ultimately exempt one from the finality of death; the other is the belief in the existence of an all-powerful rescuer. These provide the protection one needs to participate in the healthy denial of one's finality. These modes of denial come under continued challenge when one is assaulted by the raw reality of multiple deaths. Thus, the ability of the therapist or helping professional to use denial adaptively may fail, resulting in the onset of helplessness, hopelessness, and despair. These reactions are not necessarily prompted solely by death witnessing but by the limits on the therapist's ability to provide significant relief from the overwhelming emotional distress that many patients experience. They constitute subjective countertransference reactions since there is no evidence that the therapists or group practitioners use these feelings to inform themselves of the clients'/group members' emotional states.

Helplessness

Helplessness is defined as an experience of powerlessness, impotence, or defenselessness generated by the perception that a particular aversive event cannot be controlled, alleviated, or remedied. In psychological theory, helplessness is often associated to a trauma, traumatic stress reactions, and depressive states (Bibring, 1953; Farber, 1994; Seligman, 1975). Intense and painful emotions and psychological concerns experienced by many persons with AIDS present formidable clinical challenges for therapists in the arena of helplessness. Feelings of helplessness, weakness, self-doubt, uncertainty, and insecurity are intimately associated with the practitioner's struggle to facilitate emotional relief in the PWA. The emergence of such feelings may be contradictory to the therapist's ideal sense of self as helpful, empowering, and comforting.

Farber in his 1994 study of helplessness in AIDS therapists observed that the acknowledgment of helplessness may enable the therapist to be more helpful.

> The exercise of acknowledging feelings of helplessness to oneself also may help to ameliorate the risk of such countertransference responses as avoidance or withdrawal from the patient, minimization of patient distress, overreaction to patient distress or anger toward the patient . . . therapist openness to countertransferential responses of helplessness is apt to increase the likelihood that patients can be helped to understand their feelings and reactions, identify maladaptive coping patterns, and explore alternative modes of coping with that distress. (p. 70)

Helplessness is ultimately linked to feelings of envy, rage, and hatred. Therapist rage may emerge as an outgrowth of these feelings of helplessness, as well as from narcissistic injury, i.e., injury to therapeutic zealousness (Rosenthal, 1987) and/or omnipotence (Renneker, 1957), or as aim attachment countertransference reaction (Slavson, 1953). As such, the helplessness-rage connection may be understood in the following manner:

[We] are willing to give, understand, and be helpful, but we expect something back as a reward. What may be a major distinction between one therapist and another is what and how much he can give and what and how soon he expects something back from his patient . . . there is no better way to bring it out in us than in our work with a patient who repeatedly tells us he is helpless and hopeless, and demonstrates repeatedly that our giving is not enough, or valueless, or non-existent, even minutes after it was previously acknowledged, and that ultimately all our giving attempts are rejected and destroyed. (Adler, 1972, p. 319)

In the context of psychotherapy with PWAs, the concept of wanting something back such as the therapeutic success with PWAs is very complex, because in spite of the therapist's best efforts, many clients die and often with their death goes the feeling of failure. Any success feelings may be contaminated and ultimately linked with loss and a sense of survivor's guilt. To have successful feelings about therapeutic work with a client/group member who ultimately dies appears to be a complex issue having to do with the way we measure the therapeutic expertise, therapeutic success, and ourselves. Thus the practitioner working with people with AIDS is often left with feelings of helplessness and a deep sense of unfinished business. Perhaps this is in part because of the unfinished lives of those who died so young. In those instances where the patient rejected and demeaned the help, the AIDS practitioner has more opportunity to experience a full range of feelings. In those cases, the practitioner may find relief in such reactions and gravitate toward a PWA who permits him or her to have rage over feelings of helplessness.

Envy, Anger, and Rage

Although Adler (1972) and Norton (1963) noted the envy that medically ill patients may feel toward the assumed healthy therapist, little attention has been given to states of envy, anger, and rage in the literature on work with PWAs either in individual or group modalities. In countertransference, envy, anger, and rage can be both subjective and objective states. Often as objective countertransferences, envy and rage take the form of projective identification and, as such, are difficult to identify and assess. Anger, on the other hand, tends to be projected or turned inward and fuels a whole series of countertransference reactions more reliably identified by the practitioner. When first mentioned in the countertransference literature on work with people with AIDS (Dunkel and Hatfield, 1986), anger was conceptualized as a subjective countertransference reaction fueled by feelings of helplessness and culminating in a "blame the victim" scenario. As these authors observed, such anger on the part of the therapist had two functions: the first involved an attempt (albeit unconscious) to punish the PWAs; the second involved the use of anger to distance the therapist from the client as a form of self-preservation. In both instances, anger may be viewed as subjective and having more to do with the therapist's reactions to the client. If these authors observed an objective aspect to the therapist's anger, they did not report it. However, there are some PWAs whose character, temperament, and perhaps even perception of illness does not permit feeling and/or expression of anger at either their situation or those identified as their helpers. Instead, their anger is often projected much in the way Alder discusses envy and hate.

COUNTERTRANSFERENCE PHENOMENA IN PWA SUPPORT GROUPS

Clearly, countertransference reactions such as these are ever present in support groups. Their content, shape, and form are legion, given the sheer number of members, the nature of their individual personalities, their stage of illness, and their particular relationship to the group as a whole and to the facilitators. In contrast to individual work with a PWA, the group facilitator is confronted with members at various stages of the disease, thereby prompting a range of responses, some subjective and others objective but all requiring attention. In one group there may be a new member in the throes of coping with the first AIDS infection; another member may be talking about his steady deterioration from a new OI; another may be approaching a later course in the illness, struggling with her fears of making plans for herself and her children; yet another member may be preoccupied with discouragement over the rejection by a drug protocol for long-term survivors. Each member will evoke both subjective and objective countertransference reactions in the facilitator, and each of these reactions will also converge, creating a group-as-a-whole countertransference.

Death Anxiety, Contagion, and Helplessness as Subjective and Objective Countertransference Reactions

A number of group practitioners provide illustrations that highlight how difficult it is for the group practitioner to tolerate feelings of helplessness, especially in groups for PWAs. States of helplessness appear to precipitate behaviors in the therapist including "action mode" (Tunnell, 1991), "rescuing" (Herman, 1992), "jumping in" (Bernstein and Klein, 1995), and "actions of the helpless" (Gabriel, 1991). Tunnell, remarking on the power of helplessness in AIDS group therapists, calls attention to the message given to the group member and the group as a whole when the therapist can neither tolerate nor contain feelings of helplessness:

> [The] specific way in which therapists lose objectivity is that the extreme emotional experience of AIDS patients tends to induce in the countertransference feelings of helplessness. Facilitating an AIDS group evokes the therapist's own feelings of inadequacy, ineffectiveness and helplessness—feelings that are rarely as powerful in other psychotherapy groups . . . As with other countertransference reactions therapists need to discuss their feelings with other therapists and supervisors as well as utilize those feelings to understand group dynamics. If instead therapists act on the feelings by rushing in to "save" or "protect" the patient, a message gets conveyed that the patient is inadequate . . . Moreover, a more harmful message is conveyed that the therapist cannot bear listening to what the patient is saying. (pp. 495–96)

In the literature on groups with PWAs, the countertransference reactions stimulated around death of group members appeared more directly related to death anxiety in therapists. Tunnell (1991) referred to early death and Gabriel (1991) referred to first death in a group as crucial to the group's development. Death anxiety may also serve as a trigger for a range of countertransference reactions in the group facilitators—some subjective and others clearly objective. In the example to follow, a range of countertransference reactions is expressed: death anxiety, contagion, and helplessness. In this vignette a group therapist is telling her own supervision group about the death of one of the members in the support group she is facilitating:

We had our first death this week. I didn't know what to do and at one point I didn't know what I felt. I didn't do anything with it yet in my group. It is so hard to believe that B. is dead. He had so much life. All through our group today, I thought any minute now B. will arrive and make a grand entrance and then regale us with stories. . . . anyway what I did with the group about the death was not to call and tell them. If they saw it in the paper that was one thing: if they hear from each other, well, that was another. Maybe the family called someone in the group as well. I didn't think to ask. So when the group started I waited to see if anyone would mention B. No one did. They were going to avoid bringing it up. I felt I couldn't sit through the whole session without acknowledging B. was dead. It was not possible even if it was good practice to wait. I couldn't do it. Besides, I don't think it is good practice. So about 15 minutes into the group session, I said, "I have some bad news. Are people ready for bad news?" Some said they were and some said they were not. So this was discussed for a while. Finally they agreed they wanted to hear. I finally said B. had died. They were shocked. I was shocked again. They asked how and when and where. But interestingly no one asked about the funeral. In fact, after a few minutes they went back to talking about other things. Then one member said he couldn't believe how we were all avoiding B.'s death. I think he was including me and he should have. They talked about it some more and then moved on. . . . I still don't know how I will deal with the next death. I am not sure this experience has taught me anything about dealing with death. (Gabriel, 1991, p. 285)

In retrospect, it is clear that the group facilitator's dilemma about telling the members about B.'s death at the group meeting spoke to her own subjective countertransference to his death, as well as to the induction from the group. The group both wanted and did not want to know. Their ambivalence was clearly captured in their approach—avoiding talking about B.'s death, mirroring the facilitator's behavior of telling/not telling.

As Tunnell (1991) suggests,

bereavement in AIDS groups is necessarily complicated by the fact that the survivors share the same diagnosis and prognosis as the deceased. For some members, the event of an early death may cause the group itself to become symbolic of death instead of life, with the consequence that the attractiveness of the group to its members is severely thwarted, just at a time in other therapy groups when cohesion is increasing. (pp. 484 & 485)

The group may be a symbol of death not only for the members but for the facilitators as well. In studying and grappling with powerful feelings, the facilitators need to scrutinize their own subjective responses to the experience in/of the group, as well as to search for feelings held and induced by the group. For some practitioners, this first death or sudden death of a member may precipitate an existential crisis or moment leading them to a rigorous examination of their beliefs regarding death, circumstances of their own death, and ultimately issues of aloneness. All their experiences with death are finally woven into the tapestry of their counter-transference reactions. And what is emphasized is the subjective nature of the experience.

Envy and Rage as Subjective and Objective Countertransference Reactions

There are instances in which facilitators observe a cohesiveness among group members. Thus, they may begin to think and talk about their group as having a sense of cohesion. They may, in fact, be tremendously relieved that in the midst of deterioration and death, members are achieving a connection with one another. Such a sense of relief may eclipse the therapist's vision regarding the presence and depth of cohesion in the group. In fact, the therapist's premature or wishful emphasis on positive regard and a feeling of "we-ness" may mask a split in the group. In the following example, the facilitators relate how they attempted to introduce the notion of a new member into a highly "cohesive" group that, not long before, had experienced the death of two members. The bereavement following the deaths appeared to the facilitators to have increased group cohesion. In introducing the idea of a new member, the facilitators were aware that members might view the newcomer as an attempt to replace old members. All possible reactions to the facilitators' intention of introducing a new member were discussed, along with the revisiting of feelings surrounding the lives of the two members who had died some six or seven months ago. Despite careful exploration, the group became enraged, fighting among themselves while differing about all the reasons it was unwise to bring in a new member. The facilitators became enraged with the group's agreed-upon motto, "no new members." In the following, these facilitators discuss their group members' reactions in a supervision group session:

> It's so annoying, why do they protest so? Maybe we should let it go for now. We have asked every possible question. They clearly said: "If new members are accepted, some of us will leave." It is so enraging. I mean, it is more work to have new members on the one hand, while on the other it would enhance and liven up the group. Why would they be so against us having a new member? Eventually we will have to add members. We may just have to override them. But I feel so angry. I hate them, I really do. They are entitled and negative!

It was when the facilitators were finally able to ask the group whether their objection to a new member had to do with fear of getting a "sicker" member that the members were finally able to verbalize their resistance and the reasons they opposed and felt so rageful toward the facilitators. They revealed how angry they were at "them"—*the facilitators,* the healthy ones who would ultimately be the long-term survivors of the group. Their anger was expressed in the form of questions about the facilitators' motives, statements about the facilitators' freedom to come and go from AIDS, comments about the facilitators not having to cope with the illness, and suggestions that the facilitators were using the group to learn from them about the illness. As their strong differences emerged around the different sources of their anger toward the facilitators, the formerly perceived cohesiveness of the group dissipated as members behaved more assertively and aggressively toward each other as well as toward the facilitators.

In this instance the facilitators' anger was a clue to objective countertransference reactions here; that is, as Adler (1972) observed, the group's "hate" was in large part aroused because they were to be guided and assisted in their illness by facilitators whom they viewed as physically well. The cohesiveness the facilitators thought they observed following the two members' deaths might be better understood as an "anxious clinging together" (Molnos, 1990). The group members thus may have been unable to tolerate their ambivalent feelings toward one another and the facilitators. The good feelings were split off from the bad and the bad displaced upon the suggested new member, a reality, i.e., a new member, located outside the room. Only in splitting in this manner could the group tolerate one another and the deaths of two of its members. Only when the facilitators persisted in exploring the resistance to the new member did the anger become open and expressed. It appears that this mechanism of splitting is very common in these groups, perhaps owing to regression in ego functioning of the members as a consequence of the traumatic experience of confronting many different infections, death, grief, and other stressful psychological and physical states. Many of these group dynamics reflect the constellation of ego splitting that induces in the facilitators unwanted, unacceptable, unspoken feelings.

Fears of Contagion

Contagion understood as a psychological as well as a biological process greatly influences all AIDS practitioners. It is a ubiquitous phenomenon in all AIDS groups, though it is rarely discussed. Perhaps only with regard to drug-resistant TB do group members begin to struggle with the most concrete manifestations of contagion in the world of AIDS. As such, contagion appears to be a form of death anxiety and thus may be responded to with an array of defense mechanisms, especially denial.

The fear of contagion presents as a subjective countertransference reaction in group therapists. Their conscious recognition of these fears often serves as a source of shame, embarrassment, and guilt. These feelings complicate the understanding of the role of contagion in AIDS work (Field and Shore, 1992; Namir and Sherman, 1989; Molnos, 1990).

The group practitioner Scott Sherman (1989), reflecting on his experience of countertransference in his PWA group, speaks of one of his two experiences of feelings of contagion:

> The first was leading a therapy group as part of a research project with 12 men who had AIDS. Following the group, they were asked to fill out some forms. Many of the men did not have pens; I happily loaned out mine for them to use. After everyone had finished and left the room, I was left with the pen several men with AIDS had used, and I did not know what do with it. I threw the pen out, fearful of even touching it. I realize now that I was overwhelmed by the experience of so many ill, dying men who were not very different from myself. . . . In my anxiety about having to deal with issues and fears about death and dying, I could not touch them—either physically or emotionally—not even a pen they had touched (Namir and Sherman, 1989, p. 275).

As described above, the fear of contagion appears to be closely related to death anxiety and symbolizes the therapist's expression of anxiety in this regard. Molnos (1990), a British group analyst writing on the healing and destructive power of groups in HIV work, suggests that AIDS triggers "in all of us an archaic animal fear" (p. 44). She describes the "blind terror" she experienced after shaking hands with a PWA whom she encountered for the first time. Subsequent to this event she reported her reactions:

> It produced a ridiculously surrealistic dialogue in my head. The dialogue was so vivid that subsequently I could write it down. He and his destiny occupied my mind as I was going home. . . . At the same time panicky sentences started crossing my mind in rapid succession: "Don't touch anything!" "Concentrate, don't touch your face!" "Oh, my God," "How will I eat? I cannot touch any food." On my arrival home I washed my hands with soap. I washed them twice and that was it. The whole phenomenon disappeared without further trace. . . . The above experience left me disconcerted, ashamed of myself, my self-image shattered by the close encounter with a blind ancestral animal in me. (p. 46)

For Molnos this whole experience lasting some twenty minutes symbolized the power of blind, primitive terror associated with AIDS and the fear of contagion. It illustrates how overwhelmed a perfectly well-informed and rational mind can become when confronted with death anxiety. In studying and discussing her reactions, Molnos suggested that such a fear of contagion, of "blind terror," as she prefers to call it, contains the following components: simultaneous presence of the irrational and the rational, feelings of being split inside oneself or being torn apart by two opposite forces, and the sudden appearance and the equally abrupt disappearance of the whole experience.

All the group practitioners reporting such fears of contagion focus on the shame, guilt, and embarrassment associated with these experiences. Group practitioners not infrequently though hesitantly reveal that they fear to use the telephone, bathroom, coffee cups, and pens handled by PWAs, while commenting that they are well aware that these are not sources of transmission. Even after lengthy training in infectious diseases carried by hospital personnel repeatedly emphasizing the transmission modes, mental health practitioners, especially those who see PWAs in individual or group modalities, continue to struggle with issues of contagion. This suggests that contagion as a countertransference is both difficult for the practitioner to identify and even more difficult to discuss with colleagues or supervisors. If therapists have such strong fears of contagion, one can only speculate what it must be like for the PWA to sit in a room with six or eight other PWAs, each with compromised immune systems and some more symptomatic than others. Surely they must have this same "blind terror." If so, should there be a time to talk about this terror? How are they to do this, if those who facilitate such groups are themselves blocked by their own terror in giving words to the unspeakable? It is important to emphasize that the powerful presence of these irrational states may provoke in the group practitioner as well as in the group a set of behaviors that are focused on denying the existence of this fear. These derivative behaviors may be the ones that create avoidance of the topic of contagion.

Identification as an Objective and Subjective Countertransference Reaction

Identification with the group or group member's story, feelings, circumstances, wishes and fantasies, the concordant identifications and identification with the members' perceptions of past relationships or feelings toward others in their lives, and the complementary identification are ever present in all forms of group practice. In some instances these identifications make for powerful countertransference reactions. As Loeser and Bry (1953) noted, the major source of countertransference in group therapies is the group practitioner's identification with a member, members, or the group as a whole. The difficulty arises as a result of excessive identification with a group member, which may eventuate in the facilitator's "duplicating" the feeling states of the member with such intensity that the group practitioner is unable to "snap out of" this identification and thereby merges to some degree. The result is the therapist's recognition of the member as a unique and separate entity. Under such circumstances this would be regarded as a subjective countertransference reaction. Group practice with PWAs is rich in examples of these kinds of countertransference responses because of the sheer impact of the numbers of members available for identification, the degree of death anxiety induced in a group setting where one is confronted with a number of medically ill persons. The fear of contagion and the helplessness associated with these kinds of groups create a regressive emotional pull for the facilitators that may prompt instantaneous overidentifications and merger with the members. In these instances the use of these identifications for greater understanding of the members' plight is substantially diminished. The example offered below provides a view of the identification as a subjective countertransference that could be used objectively to provide information about the member's behavior in the group.

Eva, a young Hispanic woman estranged from her extended family since disclosure of her AIDS diagnosis, has talked frequently in the group about her two daughters, 8 and 10 years old, who are HIV seronegative. One of the group facilitators, H., has repeatedly intervened with Eva, calling her attention to her need to plan for these two children in the event of her further disability and possible death. All of these attempts were "ineffective," according to H. and her co-facilitator. Instead these were arousing splits in the group with some members joining the facilitator in trying to pressure Eva to do some planning. What was revealed in the course of group supervision with these facilitators was H.'s intense identification with Eva. She, like Eva, has two children and like Eva was estranged from her family. She, however, has worked out a careful custody arrangement excluding her family. The countertransference identification she had was to Eva's situation having to do with Eva's relationship to her family and children. A "fixed" identification with these circumstances precluded H. from exploring or assisting the group in exploring why Eva thought as she did in this matter. If H. had been able to "snap out" of this identification with Eva, she may have been free to use this identification to explore Eva's relationship to her family and her children. In this instance the identification drew her attention to an important element in Eva's behavior but H. was unable to use it in understanding Eva.

The power of identification as a countertransference reaction is awesome. In full force it effectively halts any dialogue or effective storytelling, because for however long it lasts the facilitator and the member or the group as a whole are merged and in some sort of narcissistic joining that precludes communication, especially exploration communications: "What is the thinking here?" "What effect does this have on you or the group?" "What stops you from thinking about these matters and talking about them here?" "Should the group be helping you to think about these matters?" All these questions remain unasked because their answers are assumed by virtue of identification.

SUMMARY

In this chapter definitions and illustrations of countertransference were provided from its first conceptualization to its current understanding emphasizing the various elaborations on the concept, first as it is understood in individual psychotherapy and then in group psychotherapies, focusing on two aspects of countertransference reactions—the subjective and the objective. Attention was then given to the general area of countertransference reactions in therapists to those with medical illness. Then the focus was on therapists, both individual and in group, for those with HIV and AIDS. To highlight the countertransference reactions that may be encountered in support group therapy, several of the more frequently observed reactions such as death anxiety, fear of contagion, helplessness, envy, anger, and rage were discussed and illustrated. Ultimately it became clear that in the current arena of groups with PWAs, the focus is heavily on identification of subjective countertransference reactions. Little if any attention has been given to the objective aspects of these reactions as a method of informing the group practitioners of yet unverbalized feelings. As more and more practitioners give voice to their observations, the objective countertransference may find greater mention in group literature and ultimately in group practice with people with AIDS.

CHAPTER 5

Secondary Traumatic Stress Reactions in AIDS Group Practitioners

Burnout, Vicarious Traumatization, Compassion Fatigue, Survivor Psychology

In this chapter, we examine the impact of facilitating an AIDS support group on the group practitioner. Clearly, the group practitioner in an AIDS-related practice is bombarded by a host of special circumstances that appear specific to AIDS work: early deaths of young men and women, stigma and discrimination, issues of contagion, issues of group fragmentation due to frequent illnesses, a group member's shifting health status, and changes in a member's mental status. In light of such special circumstances, the facilitator needs to be prepared to assume shifting roles and functions, i.e., hospital or home visitor, advocate with family and medical facilities, attendance at funerals and memorials. Simultaneously, facilitators are confronted with such clinical issues as rational suicides, dementia, multiple-drug-resistant TB, and a host of

135

difficulties related to the establishment and maintenance of confidentiality and group cohesiveness. For the group facilitator, subjective and objective countertransference reactions are likely to run the gamut, from death anxiety, helplessness, survivor's guilt, identification, contagion to issues of their own and their members' bias about homosexuality, race, class, gender, and/or chemical dependence. All these forces have a cumulative impact on the group practitioner. This cumulative effect is the substance of this chapter.

Beginning with the concept "burnout" (Freudenberger, 1974; Maslach, 1976), we note that there has been an ever-increasing interest in identifying the impact of therapeutic work on the practitioners in human service professions. In trauma work, such interest has given rise to conceptualizations like soul sadness (Chessick, 1978), caregiver's plight (Weisman, 1981), secondary catastrophic stress reactions (Figley, 1983), vicarious traumatization (McCann and Pearlman, 1990), compassion fatigue (Joinson, 1992), and secondary traumatic stress (Figely, 1995). Each of these concepts speaks to the effects of trauma work on the trauma practitioner, either in individual or in group work.

BURNOUT

The term "burnout" was coined by Freudenberger in the early 1970s to describe the phenomenon he observed in staff members at a "free clinic" that was providing a range of services to a medically indigent community in California. His definition of burnout—"to fail, wear out, or become exhausted by making excessive demands on energy, strength or resources" (p. 159)—essentially captured the exhaustion experienced by these health care providers. This term "burnout," used interchangeably with "stress" and "job stress," quickly entered the human professions services, giving rise to numerous articles and studies by professional and popular writers.

According to Maslach (1982), a significant contributor to the theory of burnout and the creator (Maslach and Jackson, 1982) of a standardized measurement for burnout (Maslach Burnout Inventory), there is no single definition of burnout. There is, however, certain agreement about some of the significant elements of burnout, which include emotional exhaustion, depersonalization, and reduced personal accomplishment. Emotional exhaustion in Maslach's understanding refers to a depletion of one's emotional resources and the feeling that one has nothing left on a psychological level to give to others. The depersonalization phase of burnout involves the development of negative and callous attitudes about the people one works with. A depersonalized perception of others may lead one to judge them as somehow deserving of their troubles; this mentality or attitude is called "blaming the victim." Factors that contribute to a high degree of burnout include the time spent in direct care, which may contribute to a greater risk of emotional exhaustion; the nature of the patient's health problems, especially problems that entail a high level of helplessness; and the expectations of success and failure the professional may harbor about this work. High burnout as described by Maslach occurs more often in health professionals early on in their careers, when they have repeated encounters with what they perceive as failure and thus develop a learned helplessness about their work and its impact.

Burnout in AIDS Literature

The AIDS literature also reflects an interest in the phenomenon of burnout (Bennett, Kelaher and Ross, 1994; Garside,
1993; Klonoff and Ewers, 1990; Oktay, 1992; Volberding,
1989; Wade and Simmon, 1993). Acknowledging that AIDS
has additional factors that may contribute to health professional stress, i.e., untimely deaths, absence of cures, infectious
nature of the disease, and the complex legal and ethical issues,
these writers have attempted to identify, as well as suggest interventions intended to alleviate or interrupt, the syndrome of
burnout among AIDS professionals of all disciplines.

Bruce Garside (1993), writing on his year-and-a-half facilitation of a physician mutual aid group, identified several
themes of "burnout." These primary care AIDS physicians reported helplessness, anger, and job dissatisfaction. Particularly
stressful to this group was witnessing the deaths of young
AIDS patients, as well as enduring the stigmatization they
themselves experienced from colleagues and the medical
community-at-large. Intense identification with their patients
contributed to the rage and resentment they experienced in
response to the way they perceived their AIDS patients being
treated and cared for in hospital settings.

Juliana Oktay, in her 1992 study of burnout in hospital social workers who worked with AIDS patients, reported a
higher incidence of burnout in hospital-based AIDS social
workers as compared with other hospital-based social workers. These AIDS social workers scored particularly high on
emotional exhaustion and depersonalization subscales of
burnout and low on the subscale of personal accomplishment.
Such studies suggest that although AIDS work may be per-

sonally and professionally gratifying, its price may involve a higher risk of burnout.

Bennett, Kelaher, and Ross (1994), in the course of developing a scale for measuring the impact of AIDS work on health care professionals, identified three dimensions: discrimination and stigma felt because of working with AIDS, identification with and responsibility for people living with AIDS, and grief and powerlessness associated with working with AIDS patients. These dimensions appeared to identify the areas of expressed difficulty for professional AIDS care providers.

Although burnout literature includes sophisticated qualitative and quantitative studies of this phenomenon as well as various methods to assess and measure the existence of burnout in human service providers, it offers little in the way of a specific framework for understanding burnout reactions in the context of the uniqueness of AIDS work. What appears absent is an understanding that encompasses the group practitioner's exposure to "horror" and multiple deaths, two fundamental features of this kind of trauma work and not specific to the condition of burnout.

Thus, what is called for, if the experience of AIDS practitioners is to be addressed, is a conceptualization of burnout that includes linkages to trauma concepts and observations of the impact of trauma material on professionals. Given the traumatic implications of an AIDS diagnosis and the biopsychosocial sequelae of infection, medical intervention, emotional upheaval, and confrontations with death and the dying process, what is necessary is a framework for examining the reactions of the group practitioners inclusive of the particular features of both AIDS and group intervention.

As noted in both professional and popular literature, the category of traumatized individuals or groups extends beyond those who were involved in the "actual traumatic event" to those who have survived and/or witnessed a traumatic event or events (Figley, 1995). An excellent illustration of this can be found in a newspaper report (Palmer, 1993) on the post-traumatic stress experienced by the female nurses in Vietnam in the late 1960s some twenty-five years later. As one of these nurses acknowledged, "I didn't feel I deserved to have PTSD [post-traumatic stress disorder]. I wasn't in combat" (*New York Times Magazine*, November 7, 1993, p. 72). Yet these veterans of bedside "horror" continued to suffer the ravages of their experience in flashbacks, nightmares, depression, denial, isolation, survivor's guilt, and rage. These are symptoms consonant with those reported by veterans in combat (Lindy, 1988).

Increasing interest in the psychological effects of trauma has brought into sharper focus the potential enduring psychological consequences for individual and group work therapists vicariously exposed to traumatic experiences through the narratives of their patient/clients or group members.

In fact, McCann and Pearlman (1990) suggest:

Persons who work with victims may experience profound psychological effects, effects that can be disruptive and painful for the helper and can persist for months or years after work with traumatized persons. We term this process "vicarious traumatization" . . . It is our belief that all therapists working directly with trauma survivors will experience lasting alterations in their cognitive schemes having a significant impact on the therapist's feelings, relationships and life. (pp. 133, 136).

Vicarious traumatization as described by these authors refers to the cumulative transformation effect on the therapist working with survivors of traumatic events. Although discussed here in the context of work with PWAs, this phenomenon was first identified in trauma workers, including emergency medical workers, fire fighters, police, criminal defense lawyers, battered women's homeless shelter staff, sexual assault workers, suicide hotline personnel, trauma researchers, clergy, journalists, and all others who bear witness to trauma and/or listen to trauma narratives. McCann and Pearlman suggest that as a result of this exposure to the realities of trauma, therapists are changed. This change is referred to as a transformation for group practitioners as a consequence of the empathetic engagement with the group member's trauma material. In AIDS-related work the group practitioner is exposed to the death anxiety, fear of contagion, survivor's guilt, and helplessness of witnessing events that ultimately may take a member's life. As a process, vicarious traumatization often results in repeated experiences of the helpless individual witnessing trauma, an experience that is in itself traumatic (Herman, 1992).

Vicarious Traumatization as Differentiated from
Countertransference Reactions

Countertransference reactions, as already described in Chapter 4, occur in all forms of therapy as both unconscious and conscious responses to patients, clients, or group members. Vicarious traumatization, on the other hand, is specific to therapies with people who have been traumatized. It is not a state that one "snaps out of," as in countertransference (Kernberg, 1964) but rather a process in which there is an accumulation of trauma experiences that permanently transforms the psyche of the practitioner. Countertransference is usually temporarily and temporally linked to a particular event—issues of the moment in the therapeutic experience. According to McCann and Pearlman (1990) and Pearlman and Saakvitne (1995), vicarious traumatization results in profound disruptions in the therapist's frame of reference of his or her basic sense of identity, worldview, and spirituality.

Secondary Traumatic Stress Reactions

Charles Figley (1983), a pioneer trauma theorist, provides another model for examination of the impact of AIDS support group work on facilitators. His work suggests that the group facilitator may experience a secondary traumatic stress reaction, also referred to as compassion fatigue. Through his studies of the effects on families of catastrophic events, Figley has included family, friends, acquaintances, and mental health professionals in the traumatization cycle, suggesting a secondary traumatic stress syndrome and a secondary traumatic stress disorder:

> The same kind of psychosocial mechanism within families that makes trauma "contagion" that creates a context for family members to infect one another with their traumatic material operates between traumatized clients and therapists. (p. 144)

Figley differentiated secondary traumatic stress from burnout. While he understood burnout as emerging over time and as a result of emotional exhaustion, he viewed secondary traumatic stress (compassion fatigue) as emerging suddenly. It is characterized as similar to the reactions seen in primary traumatic stress. The stressor is the trauma narrative, and the reaction in the therapists or, in this instance, group practitioners follow the similar course of traumatic stress: re-experiencing the traumatic event, avoidance/numbing of reminders of the events, and persistent hyperarousal. He suggests that these acute secondary stress reactions may last a month. Those not manifesting these reactions until six months or so would be seen as having a delayed secondary traumatic stress reaction. These elements taken collectively may best explain the general effects of trauma material on trauma workers. It may be the closest to describing the traumatization experienced by some AIDS professionals, and as such it may indicate an expansion of the concept of burnout to include those who have witnessed trauma or have been exposed to trauma narratives.

THE UNFOLDING OF VICARIOUS TRAUMATIZATION AND SECONDARY TRAUMATIC STRESS REACTIONS IN GROUP FACILITATORS

Of all those writing on the effects of trauma material on the trauma worker, perhaps the observations of Robert J. Lifton (1979) best illuminate the process of secondary traumatic stress reactions and vicarious traumatization. Basing his research on numerous explorations and interviews with primary survivors of Nazi death camps (1970), Hiroshima (1968), Vietnam (1973)—and the natural disaster of the Buffalo Creek flood (1976), Lifton identified certain themes that have been repeatedly woven through the survivor's experiences.

This concept of survivorship is a crucial aspect of AIDS work, particularly of AIDS support group therapy, because in these group settings group facilitators often become the "sole survivor" and "lone" survivor of their group. Time after time they have witnessed the dwindling of their group's membership as a consequence of debilitating illness and death. Eventually all the members of their original group, perhaps started two years earlier, are deceased. It is perhaps these issues of survivorship that ultimately translate into a survivor identity for facilitators and contribute most often to the vicarious traumatization and secondary traumatic stress reactions experienced as a consequence of this work. As Lifton states:

> An exploration of the psychology of the survivor is crucial to understanding such trauma. The study of adult trauma and survival has direct bearing on issues around death and death imagery in ways that shed a great deal of light on both psychiatric disturbances and on our own contemporary historical condition. (Lifton, 1979 p. 163)

In Lifton's conceptualization, understanding the psychology of the survivor helps tease out those elements which characterize a traumatic syndrome. The survivors, in this instance AIDS group facilitators, have come into contact with death on a psychic level or directly (if they are themselves diagnosed with HIV/AIDS) and have so far remained alive. Lifton identifies five characteristic themes in the survivor that can be applied to the experience of the AIDS group practitioner: recipient of the death imprint, perception of death guilt, state of psychic numbing, experience of nurturance as counterfeit, and struggles with the meaning of their survival as well as death.

Death Imprint

The death imprint consists of the radical intrusion of an image-feeling or threat of actual impending death. By this definition, death imprints are made in instances of prematurity, grotesqueness, or absurd death scenes. This death imprint refers to "indelible images." For Nazi death camp survivors, the imagery included smells of smoke and/or smell of the gas chambers. Vietnam veterans reported images of buddies blown apart. Often, one particular set of images crystallized around an experience of what Lifton termed "ultimate horror." For one Vietnam veteran it was the "white bone of an arm." In the Buffalo Creek disaster, a survivor's death image was of "black water." In the case of a five-year veteran group facilitator, the death image entailed the "wasted away face" of one of his group members.

> For me, AIDS will always be in the wizened face of J. His beautiful eyes sunken and filled with terror and bewilderment. He always looked bewildered although he never knew what was happening to him. Always he seemed to be in terror. I can see his face. Sometimes when I am about to fall to sleep. I see his sunken eyes . . . When he came into the room I felt like he was a "walking corpse" reminding me of those pictures I saw as a child of the concentration camp survivors.

This group practitioner recounted a dream that occurred shortly after this member's death. In this dream she went to an exhibit of patients that featured eyes. In the dream, which was recurrent, the eyes resembled J.'s but looked alive and brilliant, causing her to think that the distressing and sometimes intrusive image of his eyes was receding.

Another group facilitator new to the experience of group work with PWAs talked of the "smells" he confronted on visiting the first hospitalized member of his group.

> I went into his room. He was sleeping. His breathing was heavy and his mouth was open. I noticed a terrible smell in the room. I tried to figure out what it was. Then I moved toward his bed. The smell grew worse. I suddenly realized the smell was coming from him, his breath. . . . I smelled this smell everywhere for awhile. I can't get it out of my mind. The smell is awful, just awful.

Lifton viewed death imagery as something akin to the "end of the world," the end of time and total destruction. He states:

> there can be a thralldom to this death imagery, the sense of being bound by it and of seeing all subsequent experience through its prism. The survivor may feel stuck in time, unable to move beyond that imagery, or may find it a source of death-haunted knowledge—even creative energy—that has considerable value for his or her life. (Lifton, 1979, p. 170)

Instances of this death imprint phenomenon were reported by Friedland (1989), who described a recurrent dream he had during his first year as an internist on an AIDS unit at a Bronx hospital.

> I was walking along Jerome Avenue in the Bronx at midday. I felt the vibration of the overhead subway trains, but there was no sound. Buses maneuvered through the lanes of doubled-parked cars and greengrocer stands pushed onto the sidewalk with bins of tropical fruit, but there was no color. Everything looked right and as it should have been but there were no peo-

ple; the silent, secret epidemic had carried them away. I've long since stopped having this dream, but flashes of its images sometimes break into my consciousness. (p. 61)

Similarly, group practitioners in AIDS support groups during their first few months of work and subsequent to the first death of a group member or members often reported such recurrent dreams. One group practitioner spoke at some length about a recurring dream she had following the group's visit to a sick member in the hospital.

In the dream I am walking down an alley, there is blood on the ground and I have no shoes on. My feet are cut and I think I will get AIDS. It's just as well. I might as well get it over with. I am not frightened in the dream. But when I awake, I am terrified. I know this dream was related to seeing E. in the hospital. It wasn't his condition so much, it was the hospital. The signs, the smells . . . it was the first time I really got in touch with my own terror about hospitals, illnesses and dying.

Silverman (1993) noted the expression of distress reported by health professionals working with AIDS patients as including AIDS-related nightmares, recurrent nightmares, intrusive thoughts, mental images concerning HIV-related activities, numbing, irritability, aversion to certain patients with a particular OI, physical exhaustion, and diminished interest in professional and personal activities. Such emotional responses are reported repeatedly as part of the burnout syndrome. Nightmares, intrusive thoughts, and mental images related to HIV activities appear central to the trauma aspect of this kind of work.

Survivor's and Bystander's Guilt

The second theme around which group facilitators' reactions may be examined is survivor's guilt. For Lifton, helplessness within the framework of death imagery is a significant component of survivor's guilt. More specifically, the guilt is born out of survivors' inability to act in ways they deem appropriate, i.e., either saving people or helping them. Such guilt may be compounded by the belief that one's survival is in some way related to another's death. Much of the therapeutic literature on work with terminally ill patients (Farber, 1994; Ferlic, Goldman, and Kennedy, 1979; Rennecker, 1957; Ringler, Whitman, Gustafson, and Coleman, 1981) speaks to the issue of the wellness of the health provider and the consequential guilt that arises during and after the death of the patient. This often takes the form of questions about why one survives and another dies. Instances of survivor's guilt are frequent in group facilitators, especially since they may be the lone survivor of their AIDS support group and the one left to hold all the memories for all members who have died. Danieli's (1984) concept of "bystander's guilt" and Herman's (1992) "witness guilt" may apply to the experience these practitioners are reporting. Central to Danieli's understanding of therapists' reactions to therapeutic work with Holocaust survivors is the concept of bystander's guilt, which, she believes, is reflected in such statements as "I feel an immense sense of guilt because I led a happy and protected childhood while these people have suffered so much" (p. 27). For the therapists she studied, this guilt served as a defense against the helplessness and despair evoked by the narratives of the survivor. Bystander's guilt for the therapist working with PWAs is illustrated in the following vignette:

Let's see, I've been here seven years. Isn't that right? Yes, seven years. Doing two groups a week—one an AIDS group and one a care partners. My original group, six men, is gone. All of them are dead. Dead a long time now. So I'm the only one who remembers. . . . Why do I remember? Well, I remember usually because someone in my present group reminds me of someone in that original group. My first AIDS group family as it were. I often wonder why I have been spared. So little separates me from their fate. I puzzle over it sometimes. It was different then, with that group. There was a "real" sense of community. My group members believed the epidemic would end quickly. It was a crisis and soon it would end. So there was a lot more hope in my AIDS group then. This was despite the fact they were dying very quickly. There was more hope. . . . I guess I am a "long-term survivor" of AIDS group work. I feel like I have been through so much; most of those I shared this with are dead. So surviving is a very lonely business.

Psychic Numbing

This feature of a survivor's responses termed psychic numbing (Lifton, 1979) is central to all trauma theory and is a major feature of burnout when states of depersonalization are involved (Maslach, 1982). Perhaps psychic numbing survivor response more than any other links burnout with these newer concepts of secondary traumatic stress responses. Psychic numbing refers to the diminished capacity to feel. Lifton suggests that under catastrophic circumstances, the survivor is unable to experience ordinary emotional responses. For the individual or group practitioner, listening to the narratives of PWAs during the course of their illness and bearing witness to their physical and emotional struggles may indeed constitute a catastrophic circumstance. The therapist, in response, may at times be overwhelmed by images of illness, deterioration, and death, and may assume a posture that helps him or her to ward off feelings, thus experiencing a partial deadening of feeling, dichotomizing images from feeling states. While such dissociation may result in a temporary psychological escape from horror and helplessness, as McCann and Pearlman (1990a) suggest, it may leave the practitioner with an altered perception of the self as survivor as well as an altered perception of the world. Lifton, too, makes reference to the possible long-term effects of such dissociation and numbing. He reflects on how the trauma he witnessed and the traumatic narratives he listened to as a clinical investigator affected him. Lifton's experience with the trauma framework may parallel the experiences of AIDS therapists. In describing his own responses to interviews with Hiroshima survivors (1968), he states:

> I used my investigative function to protect myself. I had undergone a certain amount of diminution of feeling, what I later came to think of as selective, professional numbing. I do not think I became insensitive to the suffering described to me, but I did develop sufficient distance from it to enable me to conduct the study. A certain amount of numbing is probably necessary in most professional situations . . . but it is surely excessive in our society and in the country . . . so great is the diminished emotion around professionalism that one sometimes wonders whether becoming a professional is not in itself part of still another devil's bargain in which one ceases to feel very much about the central most threatening questions of our time. (p. 121)

Lifton's articulated responses are perhaps best understood as "vicarious traumatization," i.e., the experience of being traumatized by and through the trauma of others. Drawing on Lifton's experience, we think it reasonable to suggest that many group facilitators who have led groups for PWAs for more than two years are particularly vulnerable to vicarious traumatization. Psychic numbing may be detected in an affectless manner of recounting events such as reporting deaths, describing hospital visits, discussing a member's physical deterioration, or recounting an experience at a funeral or memorial. A frequent manifestation of "psychic numbing," i.e., disconnection, may be in supervisory session. The following example suggests the phenomenon of disconnection. Here, the group practitioner has been facilitating an AIDS support group for less than a year.

> I don't understand this [supervision group]. We behave so differently here. At least I do. I say something that has happened in my group as when J. died, and you all sit there, say nothing and go on to someone else. Most of the time we really don't respond to each other. We just tell our tales of "horror" and move on. No one is here. Is everyone dead here, too? Is the work making us dead? I don't get what is happening. . . . How come people aren't asking me questions or showing some kind of distress with all of this? What about you [pointing to the supervisors]? Why don't you get someone to respond here?

The perception of pervasive disconnection articulated by this group facilitator is a common denominator in many supervision groups for group therapists in AIDS support group work. As such, it may be a consequence of a facilitator's desire to avoid connecting with painful affects involved in the work. This, referred to by Lifton as "professional numbing," or "vicarious traumatization" by McCann and Pearlman (1990), may, in fact, be a significant and expectable outgrowth of this work. A poignant example of this phenomenon may be heard in this group facilitator's feelings about coming to a supervision group.

> Sometimes I come here and I am so glad there is no feeling. I want a nice intellectual conversation about this work. I want to talk in detail about group interventions and what works or does not work. I do not want feelings here. I can take those to my therapist. . . . I think this supervision requires feelings and I don't have any. If I didn't have to come here I wouldn't. It doesn't help. I don't want feelings, I want direction and interventions.

Counterfeit Nurturance

The cycle of vicarious traumatization appears to include a condition referred to by Lifton (1982) as counterfeit nurturance and identified by Janoff-Bulman (1985, 1992) as shattered assumptions. This state, which appears to emerge as a consequence of the death imprint, survivor's guilt, and/or bystander's guilt, may have its origins in the psychic numbing and depersonalization responses described earlier. According to Lifton, it follows upon witnessing or directly experiencing just how unreliable human relationships can be. "The survivor," according to Lifton, "is on guard against false promises of protection, vitality or even modest assistance" (p. 1017). Janoff-Bulman provides a comprehensive conceptual structure for understanding how our assumptive world is highly impacted by experiences of trauma. As discussed in chapter two, she suggests that three assumptions are relevant to one's view of self and world: the belief in personal invulnerability, the perception of the world as meaningful and comprehensible, and the view of ourselves as positive. Each of these assumptions may be called into dramatic question in the course of this trauma work. In AIDS trauma, the stigma of the illness and the bias, prejudice, and discrimination often directed toward PWAs not only by society at large but by a PWA workplace, family, or friend may have an eroding impact on a practitioner's assumptive world. The group practitioner frequently hears narrative from the PWA enumerating the different ways the PWAs' network has been rejecting, condemning, or abandoning. Bearing witness to the rejection of father, mother, friend, colleague, child, or stranger often expressed in a PWA's conflict around whether to tell of the diagnosis has shattered for many group practitioners the notion of the durable support system. Such ruptures in the fabric of family support is sadly documented by the very existence of organizations of parents and siblings of PWAs who travel the country attempting to diminish the rejection and condemnation visited upon PWAs' family members. Such tales of rejection are profoundly troubling to the group practitioner, who, as Janoff-Bulman suggests, may hold the view that the family is a positive and sustaining force, especially in times of illness and the threat of death.

A second element in this process of counterfeit nurturance as articulated by Lifton (1979) is contagion, which is associated with the psychology of survivorhood. More specifically, survivors often feel that they are treated as carriers of the "horrors" they have witnessed:

That others view them as in some way carrying the taint of the Holocaust—as a person to be feared and avoided as though the taint were contagious. The survivor can be a reminder not only of death but of the grotesque death characteristics of the holocaust they experience. They can thus be a subject of a "second victimization." (p. 123)

This "contagious feeling" appears to constitute a familiar aspect of the group facilitator's experiences, and, not surprisingly, these feelings appear to parallel and mirror the experiences of the PWA. Since HIV is itself so intensely associated with stigma and contagion, group practitioners often feel the effects of this stigmatization. For these group therapists, the suspicion of counterfeit nurturance takes the form of feeling isolated and disenfranchised in the world of mental health professionals. Such is illustrated in the observations of a very experienced group facilitator on retiring from his PWA group:

The one drawback about this work has been the isolation. In the beginning the isolation wasn't noticeable. I would talk about my group in my supervision and the rest of the time I was careful not to say much. Then I began to notice that if I said as much as I was running an AIDS group, people would respond in some vague way and drop the subject very quickly. So that discouraged me from mentioning my work in certain circles. Then I began to be very burdened with the deaths and all the illnesses in the group, so I found myself wanting to at least speak about some of my distress, in my regular work supervision group and in my treatment group. The response from my colleagues was amazing and quite disappointing. Rather than helping me or inviting me to talk more, they would respond by saying such things as "how could you do that work?" "It sounds so depressing, how can you do it" "I couldn't do that kind of group." All these communications I heard as distancing. If I would push to tell my feelings, I often heard responses which suggest I get out of the work, not necessarily help to do the work. This was pretty much my experience through these past six years. It is very lonely. You only talk frankly and honestly about the work with others who do the work. The rest of the people, even your colleagues, seem unavailable on this topic. . . . I felt lonely but on the other hand I really bonded with my AIDS supervision group. That was the place to be. I will miss that group. But I hope I can get to feeling more attached to my other colleagues and friends. But I don't know, this work it does something to you. Sometimes it gives you the feeling of being special, especially privileged, and at other times it feels like you have no feelings anymore. That nothing surprises, impresses you or inspires you. My feelings are very mixed about it all. This is why I'm leaving now to find out what kind of person I am now without my AIDS group.

Struggle for Meaning

The fifth aspect of the cycle of vicarious traumatization for group practitioners in AIDS support groups relates to the struggle for meaning, which characterizes all the documented survival experiences. The struggle to find meaning appears to translate into the impulse to reestablish at least the "semblance of a moral universe" and an attempt to heal the shattered assumptions of a world transforming it into a place that is as meaningful and comprehensible (Janoff-Bulman, 1985). For each survivor group that Lifton studied over the past fifty years, the struggle for meaning was associated with the "impulse to bear witness." Such an impulse appears rooted in the notion that we, the living, bear some responsibility to the dead. Illustrations of bearing witness are embodied in memorials and other activities. For the Jewish community worldwide it is the establishment and maintenance of the state of Israel, for Jews in the United States it is the National Holocaust Museum in Washington, D.C., for Hiroshima survivors it is encompassed in the lifelong efforts to control the spread of atomic weapons; for Vietnam survivors it has been to claim honorable recognition via the National Vietnam War Memorial. In the PWA community the struggle for meaning has been embodied in the call to bear witness through the National Quilt Project, in organizations such as ACT-UP, and in fund-raising efforts focused around the theme of remembrance. Building on the experience of other survivors, PWAs have embraced the notion that "Silence is Death" and used the media to bring the epidemic to national awareness in a way that no other major life-threatening disease advocates have. Taken collectively, these efforts appear to reflect a struggle for meaning.

Group facilitators in PWA support groups have served as witnesses to multiple narratives about the lives of many persons with AIDS. Such witnessing has inspired profound commitment to PWAs through their therapeutic endeavor. The importance of this role for the group practitioner is captured in the observations made by a group facilitator:

For me, it is all about bearing witness. I want them to know that I heard their struggle. Maybe because so many were gay men who had never really told their story, bearing witness has more meaning. But I stayed here because my role is not only as group therapist, but also as "witness." No one will be allowed to forget Jim, Jon, Heidi or Adam. Maybe their families could erase them from their minds. But they will live in mine. Now that I have told you about them, you are all involved in the witnessing as well. . . . I take such courage from their struggle. I am a often in such admiration of how in the midst of their own illness, their own dying, they can be so helpful to others. That is the power of group. It is so incredible.

DISRUPTING THE CYCLE OF SECONDARY TRAUMATIC STRESS IN AIDS GROUP PRACTITIONERS

As increasing attention is focused on the impact of trauma work on trauma workers, a variety of interventions have been suggested and implemented for disrupting the emerging processes identified here as vicarious traumatization. Vicarious traumatization is conceptualized as shifts in the therapist's cognitive schemata resulting in heightened feelings of vulnerability, an extreme sense of helplessness or exaggerated sense of control; chronic suspicion about the motives of others; loss of personal control and sense of freedom; and chronic bitterness, cynicism, and alienation (McCann and Pearlman, 1990b), leading to states of secondary stress disorder defined by the five themes elaborated upon by Lifton (1979, 1982) in his survivor psychology. Interventions cited as useful in disrupting this cycle in practitioners working with trauma survivors may have significant relevance for group facilitators in AIDS groups. Such interventions include guided traumatic imagery (Brett and Ostroff, 1985), eye movement desensitization (Schapiro, 1989, 1995), supervision and consultation

(Gabriel, 1994), personal therapy (Perlman and Saakvitne, 1995), support groups (Grossman and Silverstein, 1993), psychodrama group (Thacker, 1984), stress reduction programs (Flannery, 1990), and meditation/spirituality (Kabat-Zinn, 1990). Other antidotes mentioned are in the realm of personal activities referred to as "healing activities" (Pearlman and Saakvitne, 1995b). These include exercise; time with family, friends, and children; journal keeping; travel; and other actions intended to reconnect trauma therapists with their mind, body, and support network.

Another emerging issue receiving growing attention in the secondary trauma stress literature is the prevention and/or disruption of secondary traumatic stress reactions in institutional settings (Catherall, 1995). Institutions such as police departments, emergency medical technicians teams, hospitals, mental health clinics, and of course AIDS programs are prone to the cycle of vicarious traumatization, causing emotional suffering for the practitioner, ineffective service, and ultimately gross financial burden to the institution.

Guided Traumatic Imagery

Guided traumatic imagery (Brett and Ostroff, 1985; Haas and Hendin, 1986) used in the treatment of post-traumatic stress disorder (Brett and Mangine, 1985; Grigsby, 1987; Stutman and Bliss, 1985) is essentially based on the psychology of "psychosynthesis" first conceptualized and refined by Roberto Assagioli (1965, 1980), who postulated that psychological distress arises from partly submerged conflict among disparate and possibly split-off aspects of the self. The imagery therapy based on these conceptualizations involves the development of an inner sense of core self partly through exploring aspects of the personality known as supersonalities, which are evoked as visual images to facilitate their gradual recognition, acceptance, integration, and synthesis. The guided images as well as nocturnal dreams create a bridge allowing unconscious ideas to become conscious by identifying and giving them form. The split-off may be the consequence of traumatic events. Three psychological processes explain the effectiveness of imagery-based therapies: the patient's feeling of control resulting from the observation and rehearsal of various images, the modified meaning or changed internal dialogue that develops, and the mental rehearsal of alternative responses that leads to enhanced coping skills (Cerney, 1985).

The role of imagery was mentioned in theoretical propositions on trauma (Freud, 1920; Ferenzci, 1924; Jung, 1928; Kardiner and Spiegel, 1947; Krystal, 1968; Horowitz, 1970). Throughout the study of post-traumatic stress there has been an emphasis of the role of images, particularly with regard to traumatic nightmares, intrusive thoughts, and flashbacks. Such events were conceptualized as overstimulation or flood of the psychic (Freud, 1920) or evidence of stress on the information processing system (Horowitz, 1970). In Horowitz's formulations (1976, 1979), based on clinical case study, experimental simulation of trauma, and interviews with traumatized persons, trauma events are viewed as new information that the individual is unable to integrate into a preexisting view of the self, others, and the world; it is information that is defensively excluded. Given the dynamic of vicarious traumatization, group practitioners may benefit from an imagery intervention that permits them the opportunity to integrate some of the distressing death and survivor imprints that may besiege them in the form of nightmares, intrusive thoughts, and flashbacks.

Imagery, Eye Movement Desensitization, and the Death Imprint

Imagery and eye movement desensitization are relatively new techniques developed in 1989 by Francine Schapiro to intervene therapeutically in post-traumatic stress disorder. The goal of eye movement desensitization (EMD) is to address a traumatic memory thought or sensation that continues to distress and preoccupy a survivor. Although it is a relatively new therapy and still a source of much professional concern and controversy, EMD is gaining the respect of a growing number of professionals as a treatment for traumatic memories. As such, it is worthy of creative consideration for those struggling with vicarious traumatization.[1] In AIDS work and particularly in AIDS group work, there is often an image or a group member or event that is "imprinted upon" the practitioner as a result of the "horror" associated with it objectively or because it symbolizes some personal experience in the practitioner's past or fantasy life. It can be the "wizened face" or the "smell associated" with a hospital visit to a dying member, or an image of a group member whose face, arms, and legs are distorted and covered with "purplish lesions" of KS, or it may be the snapshot imagery of a member who started in robust health and is now present in group demented, unkempt, and looking terrorized. A death imprint is not an unusual event in the professional life of an AIDS support group facilitator. Perhaps because of its frequent occurrence, it is not sufficiently addressed in any of the current traditional interventions.

Such interventions as guided imagery and EMD may contribute substantially to diminishing the death imprint so often associated with work with PWAs and so much a part of the experience of their group practitioners. They offer unique possibilities for enhancing the current repertoire of interventions available to assist group practitioners dealing with these imprints.

Cofacilitation and Support Groups

Cofacilitation, also known as cotherapy, coleadership, dual leadership, and joint leadership, has been referred to throughout this book as the leadership model for these support groups. Cofacilitation, a method for leading groups, was originally conceived as a context for training group practitioners (Alpher and Kobos, 1988; Gans, 1957; Roller and Nelson, 1991), and cofacilitation is currently thought of as providing certain advantages over single group leadership models. More specifically, it provides enhancement of the perception of the group therapist's self-awareness and capacity for limit setting through the presence and expertise of a second therapist (Block, 1961; Borghi, 1978; Brayborg and Marks, 1973; Demarest and Teicher, 1954; Gans, 1962); therapeutic benefits inherent in pooling the resources and abilities of both therapists (Dick, Lesser, and Whiteside, 1980; Grand, 1982; Mintz, 1963); increased possibility of therapeutic identification for members (Grand, 1982); approximation of the family context (Block, 1961; Cooper, 1976; Yalom, 1995); provision of cognitive, emotional, and physical support (Dick, Lesser, and Whiteside, 1980; Gans, 1962; MacLennan, 1965); and alleviation of isolation involved in the single facilitator leadership model (MacLennan, 1965). While all these factors support the use of the cofacilitator model, those elements that are perhaps the most important for the AIDS group practitioner are cognitive, emotional, and tangible support and the alleviation of the isolation and stigma involved in AIDS work. The support each facilitator provides the other is particularly evident during "crisis" periods in the group life, i.e., when a member is suicidal, demented, has TB, is dying or has died, or when the facilitators take on new roles such as hospital visitor and advocate. The presence of a partner means the availability of someone with whom one can share the emotional vicissitudes involved in facilitating a PWA group, develop group intervention strategies for dealing with stressful group events, and obtain assistance for addressing the day-to-day group events such as absences, follow-up calls, and pregroup interviewing. As such, cofacilitating may be a crucial factor in minimizing the traumatic impact on the cofacilitators in conducting such groups.

Of all the phenomena experienced by the cotherapy dyad, the death of a member is likely to become one of the more potent and potentially disabling events. The facilitators frequently strive to control their expression of grief in their therapy groups, citing the group's need to mourn and their belief that mourning by therapists should take place elsewhere, such as within the cotherapy relationship, in their support groups, supervision group, or personal therapy. While this position may have some merit, a cautionary note is in order. Such cordoning off of expressed feelings by the practitioner may be a contributing factor to the development of vicarious traumatization and secondary stress reactions in the practitioners, particularly those relating to states of psychic numbing. And it may serve as a model for detachment rather than attachment to the PWAs in the support group (Gabriel, 1993).

Support Groups for AIDS Facilitators

Support groups for practitioners who facilitate AIDS support groups become absolutely essential (Biller and Rice, 1990; Garside, 1993; Grossman and Silverstein, 1993; Martin and Henry-Feeny, 1989) when viewed as a place to tell one's "trauma story" and struggle with the elements of the trauma response as articulated by Lifton. As a corollary to support groups to PWAs, such groups for the practitioners are intended to provide a safe, supportive, empathic environment. As Judith Herman (1992) observes:

> Ideally, the therapist's support system should include a safe, structured and regular forum for reviewing her clinical work. This might be a supervision relationship or a peer support group, preferably both. The setting must offer permission to express emotional reactions as well as technical or intellectual concerns related to the treatment of patients with histories of trauma. Unfortunately, because of the history of denial within the mental health professions, many therapists find themselves trying to work with traumatized patients in the absence of a support context. (p. 151)

To achieve the sense of safety necessary for practitioners to talk of their alienation isolation, frustrations, helplessness, despair, and personal crises, these groups are best facilitated by a group professional not directly affiliated with the institution offering the support group. Also, it is desirable that the group professional have some training in trauma work and some exposure to the concepts of vicarious traumatization, secondary traumatic stress reactions, and compassion fatigue (Pearlman and Saakvitne, 1995a). Optimally, the group's processes need to be organized to best address the needs of members in dealing with the ongoing process of traumatization. Interventions such as imagery and EMD may be a part of the group support effort, especially in instances where practitioners are clearly struggling with issues related to the survivor concept.

Most often, these support groups for AIDS professionals become a place to mourn and deal with such phenomena as bystander's guilt, survivor's guilt, and existential and spiritual issues. Guilt and the making of meaning appear to emerge as a consequence of ongoing confrontations with illness and fears of death. What unfolds in these group sessions is a process of sharing fears and feelings associated with "bearing witness." As a result, these AIDS group practitioners perceive themselves as holding the memory of all those members who have died. In this way the struggle for meaning—one of the five elements of the survivor experience—unfolds. And it is perhaps this struggle to create meaning out of memory that contributes most to the healing process so essential in this kind of trauma work.

Supervision and Personal Therapy

Essentially, group supervision for facilitators of PWA groups is the cornerstone of a group practitioner's organized clinical training. Within this context focused information is provided, group intervention skills are taught, and mutual aid is modeled (Halperin, 1989; Leszca & Murphy, 1994; Ormont, 1980). Group supervision becomes a context not only for professional learning but a healing atmosphere where processes of vicarious traumatization in AIDS groups may be disrupted. It is here that the practitioner is encouraged to tell his or her story of and struggle within the PWA group. Fears, anticipatory anxiety about the future, anticipatory grief, and disturbing thoughts and images about group members may characterize much of the group supervision session. Accompanying the cascade of feelings often experienced by group facilitators in supervision is a preoccupation with seeking out concrete interventions and techniques from the supervisor. If these should not be forthcoming, the supervisee often becomes frustrated and distressed. This distress, if well handled by the supervisor, carries with it the potential for enhancing the group practitioners' capacity for tolerating feelings of helplessness. It provides an environment where the practitioner may tell his or her trauma story in the context of a theoretical framework. When it occurs in small-group format as suggested here, it also provides an opportunity for the group practitioner to learn group techniques by both observing and modeling how professional peers and supervisors intervene and provide support and empowerment.

In fact, Counselman and Gumpert (1993) have suggested that small-group supervision is essential to the prevention of burnout for all those doing psychotherapeutic work.

> Much of the work of a therapist is confidential and cannot be discussed ethically in general conversation. An omnipresent danger is that therapists can begin to use patients to gratify their own needs for human relationships. A supervision group provides a place not only to continue to learn, but also to let off steam, share one's anxieties, insecurities, laugh, cry and gener-

ally be with other professionals who care about each other and share concerns about the world. Therapists can experience burnout symptoms such as pervasive feelings of discouragement, incompetence or failure, anger, confusion about work and even depression. While a supervision group cannot replace good personal psychotherapy, it can help reduce clinician burnout by diminishing the isolation, confusion and shame frequently associated with it. (p. 27)

In this kind of supervision setting, the group practitioner is able to examine both objective and subjective countertransference issues related to AIDS psychotherapeutic work, i.e., death anxiety, fear of contagion, experiences of helplessness, identification, envy, anger, and projectile identification, as well as the range of thoughts, feelings, and reactions to the assumptions of the "new roles" sometimes dictated by this work. Group supervision literature is replete with illustrations of how supervision is used to highlight countertransference reactions to individual members, subgroups, and group as a whole (Adelson, 1994; Cherus and Livingston, 1993; Cooper and Gustafson, 1985; Halperin, 1989; Leszca and Murphy, 1994; Moss, 1995; Ormont, 1980).

In both the technical and emotional elements associated with this work, some aspects of psychic numbing may be addressed; that is, such examination of practitioner's work and the work of others offers the practitioner a connection to others as well as an opportunity to help colleagues. Such activities may well increase the members' capacity to feel, thereby interrupting some of the identifications with death and the dying processes that prompt this "reversible form of symbolic death" that Lifton calls psychic numbing.

Separating out and examining objective and subjective countertransference responses in group supervision occurs through a process termed "parallel process." Identification of these parallel processes as they occur in supervisory sessions requires an understanding of the theoretical propositions that this concept includes.

Parallel Process

One of the first references to parallel process was made by Harold Searles (1955) when addressing the topic of supervising those doing psychoanalytic work. Searles first labeled this process the "reflective process," suggesting that "processes at work currently in the relationship between patient and therapist are often reflective in the relationship between therapists and supervisor" (p. 135). Later Hora (1957) stressed the parallel process as an unconscious identification with the client. Hora posited that supervisees involuntarily assumed the client's tone and behaviors to convey to the supervisor and others the emotions they experienced while working with the client. It was as if the therapist were unconsciously trying in this fashion to tell the supervisor what therapeutic problems he or she was encountering (Caligor, 1981; Doehrman, 1976). In fact, given the framework of this chapter, one might speculate that parallel process may be the vehicle of vicarious traumatization discussed earlier. What is important to emphasize in this conceptualization of parallel process is that the supervisee proceeds with the presentation of factual data about patient, client, or group while unconsciously or on a nonverbal level communicating affective aspects of his or her experience. Affective communications offer clues to the supervisor and to other supervision group members who are not in the throes of induced feelings of what may be an objective or subjective countertransference response. Such replication of group process through parallel processes enables group members, as well as group supervisors, to be helpful on both cognitive and affective levels.

The theorists Wilson and Lindy (1995) have conceptualized countertransference reactions in therapists who work with persons with post-traumatic stress disorder on a continuum of Type I and Type II. In their formulations, Type I includes avoidance, counterphobic behavior, distancing, and detachment, while Type II includes overidentification, overidealization, enmeshment, and excessive advocacy. Although their framework does not include AIDS mental health practitioners, this continuum is reminiscent of the reactions often expressed and addressed in group supervision with group facilitators of PWA groups. Aspects of objective and subjective countertransference reactions are illustrated in the following vignette. In this instance, the supervision group has been meeting biweekly for two years.

> We are worried about one member of our group, Marion. She is getting more deteriorated and is making plans to move in with her mother, but she refuses to make plans like standby guardianship for her daughter. Marion was the focus of the whole session. All the members tried to influence her. She needs lots of help with this, but whatever is happening isn't enough. We have gotten exhausted with all this. Has anyone had this experience with a group member?

> Other group practitioners join in asking specific questions about this member and what the co-facilitators have said or

not said. Some had suggestions, others appeared to be interested listeners. After about forty minutes of this lengthy focus on these two facilitators, fueled by questions and suggestions, one of the supervisors asked how much time should be spent on examining one group member's behavior. Should we agree to devote the remaining hour to this? At this point one of the supervision group members said he was feeling left out. He and his co-facilitator did not have a member like this and he thought enough of the time of supervision had been spent on this group problem and it was time to move on. The two presenters became initially annoyed then apologetic, saying they were ready to move on too and were grateful for the group's help. One of the supervisors turned to another member and asked, "Is it your feeling that they got help." "No," was the reply; they just felt "cut off." "I think they felt they were taking too much time." Another member said he too "felt left out." And he wondered why the supervisors would ever suggest spending the whole time on this. At this point there was a discussion about the supervisor's intervention. Then the group facilitator who had originally brought up the issue of Marion's resistance to standby guardianship said she wondered what would have happened if she had asked this in her group. She said she had assumed they were as interested in Marion's resistant behavior as she was, and in seeing what happened here she wonders maybe it was all about her concern. Maybe, she said, it did not have a lot to do with the group's interest. Another group member said maybe it was a group resistance, they all joined it to avoid talking about themselves. Maybe another said there were other things going on in group they didn't want you to know about.

In this very brief glimpse of a supervision session, some of the complexities of the multitude of countertransference reactions are evidenced. On the one hand, this illustrates an objective countertransference and clues to a subjective countertransference. In this session these phenomena unfolded in such a way that the group facilitators have become aware of the possibility that they were induced into focusing on one member for the whole group session and were responding to the objective communications of the group as a whole, i.e., they did not want to reveal information about themselves and therefore joined in focusing on Marion. Clues to the subjective might be seen in this facilitator's keen interest in this member's responsibility to her child. Active exploration of this would be more appropriately a subject in her own personal therapy. A third phenomenon is that the repetition of a similar pattern of group behavior is taking place in the group, a parallel process alerting the supervisors to the possibility that these group practitioners are joining in focusing on two of their colleagues to avoid talking about their own groups. In this instance the supervisors chose to illustrate the countertransference reactions of focusing on one member. This intervention proved helpful to the presenting group facilitators in that they were able to see how their helplessness had in some way precipitated their taking over the group's processes. This is often the case in such groups, because the theme of helplessness is omnipresent. Such instances of identification of behaviors in the countertransference that may be prompted by helplessness provide the therapist with a way to "snap out" (Kernberg, 1964) of the countertransference and minimize the cumulative effect of the trauma material.

An area offering an abundance of countertransference reactions, both objective and subjective, is the hospital visit. For many group practitioners, as cited earlier (Namir and Sherman, 1989; Sadowy, 1991), the hospital visit is a major area of concern both from a technical and a more personal perspective, and illustrates how powerful "role shifts" can be for those working with PWAs. In the following example, reactions such as identification, distancing, survivor's guilt, contagion, and death anxiety are evidenced as one group facilitator tells his supervision group about a hospital visit to a dying group member. In a halting and tearful manner, he talks about his visit:

I think I waited too long. I went to see him when he was too close to death. But he had seemed this way before, almost dead. I decided this time I had to go. I talked to B. [co-facilitator] about going but he said he wasn't going. He has done all of the hospital visits and I think this was his way of trying to get me to do some of this work. I decided I had to go. I think it was impulsive. I knew I was beginning to be phobic about hospital visits. I hadn't visited any of the other group members [now dead] when they were in the hospital. I let B. and the group go. When I got to the hospital he really couldn't talk and he didn't seem to know I was there. I wanted to discuss my being there. I felt awkward. I felt everything I said was sort of strained. At one point he gestured for me to sit on the bed and I think he wanted me to hold his hand. This was so hard for me. . . . I felt I should go . . . maybe, to say good-bye, since I have known him for two years and he is the last of the original group. I heard from the group the next night that he died shortly after I left. It gave me a strange feeling to think that I may have been the last one to see him alive. I really don't know how I feel about the whole thing. It was so hard for me to be there. I haven't said anything to the group. I discussed it with B. and he wanted me to talk about it here. Maybe it's something others have experienced.

In this instance the practitioner was in a state of shock at the death of the group member and at his proximity to this member's death. The group facilitator identified with the group member, i.e., a young, handsome gay lawyer of similar age who had been close to the group practitioner and whom he saw regularly in the neighborhood. He felt had they not been in a professional relationship, he would have pursued a personal relationship with this member. So there was an intense countertransference reaction to him. In the group, this deceased member had played a pivotal role, often helping other members and the facilitators as well. He was respected and loved by all, including the group facilitators. His death after a long struggle and exposure to a variety of treatment interventions was viewed as valiant. For this group practitioner these events were traumatic. While he was aware of the members' dying, he also believed they would live. The death of this last member coupled with the grim and terrorizing hospital visit revealed the degree of psychic numbing he was experiencing. In retrospect, it seemed clear that this group practitioner was not sufficiently protected from his intense identification with this member, especially in view of his denial and omnipotent belief that in some way he as a group therapist would keep this particular member alive. In this instance the subjective countertransference was dominant and made the supervision group's effort ineffective.

SUMMARY

This chapter identified reactions occurring among AIDS group practitioners working with PWAs that arise as a consequence of bearing witness to events that may be perceived as horrifying. This chapter outlined and discussed the cumulative effects of AIDS work on the group practitioners by examining relatively new concepts from trauma literature, such as vicarious traumatization, secondary traumatic stress reactions, and compassion fatigue. Each of these offered some understanding of how such long-term work with PWAs in a support group context may affect the practitioner's view of self, others, and the world. The themes of survivorship, outlined by Lifton (1979, 1982), lent some understanding to how the process may actually unfold. Interventions that may diminish the effects of vicarious traumatization on group practitioners were offered. Specifically, the potential value of interventions such as guided imagery and eye desensitization movement procedures, as well as the more traditional interventions, support groups, supervision, and personal therapy, were reviewed.

Notes

Chapter 1. AIDS Trauma and Support Group Theory

1. Protease inhibitors are a new class of drugs thought to attack the
   HIV virus in ways different and more effective than previous treatments. They are enzymes that act like a chemical scissor disrupting
   the HIV replication process. In this new treatment approach, the
   goal is to offer a combination of drugs including a protease in-
   hibitor to lower the viral load and shut down HIV replication to
   the greatest degree possible. Thus far the data are hopeful. See
   Dave Gilden (1996), "Let There Be Drugs," *GMHC Treatment Issues,* 10(2), 1 & 13; and Theo Smart (1996), "Protease Inhibitors
   Come of Age," *GMHC Treatment Issues* 10(2), 3–6.
2. The perceived need for more radical political effort gave birth to
   ACT-UP (AIDS Coalition to Unleash Power). ACT-UP was created as a nonhierarchical direct action organization with the goal
   of facilitating the cure of AIDS. As a grassroots organization built
   on the concept of mutual aid and empowerment, it directed its en-
   ergies at social action on current and past AIDS-related health
   policies. It illustrates what an empowered community is able to
   achieve when it has access to power. See ACT-UP/New York
   (1991), *ACT-UP New York: Capsule History.* New York: ACT-UP.
3. The concept of empowerment has been the focus of numerous articles in major journals in community psychiatry, community psychology, social work, psychology, and nursing. Recently, as literature on women's psychological and intellectual development
   emerges, there is growing awareness that the empowerment
   process for women may be considerably different than that for
   men. Recent studies suggest that women define empowerment in
   terms of mutuality of connections with significant others, while

175

men viewed empowerment in terms of control over their environment. See J. Baker (1986), *Toward a New Psychology of Women.* Boston: Beacon Press, and J. Jordon, A. Kaplan, J. Miller, P. Stiver, and J. Surrey (1991), *Women's Growth in Connection.* New York: Guilford Press.

4. See S. Lopes (1994), *Living with AIDS: A Photographic Journal.* Boston: Little, Brown, for a pictorial review of this memorial. Officially known as the Names Project: AIDS Memorial Quilt, it was established in 1987 and grew out of community efforts to remember those who had died from AIDS. During a memorial candlelight march in San Francisco in 1985 for the late mayor, George Moscone, and the county supervisor and gay rights activist, Harvey Milk, both slain in 1978, Cleve Jones, community activist, suggested that the marchers write down the names of those who had died from AIDS that they wished to have remembered. He and others taped the names on the walls of the San Francisco Federal Building. These hundreds of squares of paper bearing the names resembled a patchwork quilt and ultimately the AIDS Memorial Quilt.

Chapter 2. Definition, Planning, Populations, and Structure
for Support Groups with PWAs

1. Bridging constitutes any group technique geared toward creating or strengthening connections between group members toward the goal of establishing a group community. See Ormont (1990, 1992b) for elaborations and illustrations of bridging techniques.

2. See M.B. Caschetta and G. Franke-Ruta (1992), Special edition women's treatment issues. *Treatment Issues: Gay Men's Health Crisis Newletter of Experimental AIDS Therapies, 6(7)* 1–27 for a complete review of HIV disease in women, including HIV effects on fertility, menstruation, and birth control. These editors also provide information of the current symptoms and treatment of syphilis, pelvic inflammatory disease, and cervical cancer.

3. The use of IV drugs is often a "social experience" whereby a person will inject in the presence of others and share the equipment of those present. This is especially true for those using IV drugs for the first time. The sharing of drugs and equipment that occurs during initial and subsequent drug use episodes leads to the notion that communal or joint use is as natural as sharing alcohol, ice, or

glasses at a cocktail party. See C. Turner, H. Miller, and M. Moses, (Eds.), (1989), *AIDS: Sexual Behavior and Intravenous Drug Use.* Committee on AIDS Research and the Behavioral, Social and Statistical Sciences, National Research Counsel. National Academy Press: Washington, D.C.

Chapter 3. *Special Issues and Considerations in Support Groups with PWAs*

1. As the incidence of HIV/AIDS continues to increase, more and more health and mental health professionals are encountering the conflict of preserving the confidentiality of a person with HIV/AIDS on the one hand while responding to the obligation to protect unsuspecting persons from the virus. See S. Erickson (1993), "Ethics and Confidentiality in AIDS Counseling: A Professional Dilemma." *Journal of Mental Health Counseling 15 (2)*, 118–131.

2. These authors observe that little is known about ways to prevent work-related infectious illnesses such as tuberculosis. They suggest that assumptions may be dangerous and expensive and pose specific questions about the effectiveness of "universal precautions" and when respirators are necessary to prevent TB exposure. In addition, they note that health care has moved from the traditional hospital settings into ambulatory, home, and other noninstitutional settings, thus increasing the complexity of worker protection measures. See L. H. Clever and V. LeGuyader, (1995), "Infectious Risks for Health Care Workers." *Annual Review of Public Health, 16,* 141–64.

3. The debate around rational suicide has been illustrated by a range of images and articles best represented by Dr. Jack Kevorkian's crusade for rational suicide, responding to the requests of those who can no longer tolerate life and in an essay by a hospice physician who writes about assisting the death of a patient. See J. Kevorkian (1991), *Prescription: Medicide: The Goodness of Planned Death.* Buffalo: Prometheus Books, and T. Quill (1994), "Physician-Assisted Death: Progress or Peril?" *Suicide and Life Threatening Behavior, 24(4),* 315–25.

Chapter 4. *Countertransference Reactions in Facilitators of PWA Support Groups*

1. See Steven Cadwell, "Empathetic Challenges for Gay Male Therapists Working with HIV-infected Gay Men." In Steven Cadwell,

Robert Burnham, and Marshall Forstein (Eds.), *Therapists on the Front Line: Psychotherapy with Gay Men in the Age of AIDS.* Washington, D.C.: American Psychiatric Press, 1994, pp. 475–96, for a thorough discussion of this concept and its relevance to the gay male therapist. It focuses on specific identification issues and the way in which these therapists managed identifications.

2. For a clinical illustration of identification of the gay therapist with a person with AIDS, see Thomas C. Rosica, "AIDS and Boundaries: Instinct versus Empathy," *Focus: A Guide to AIDS Research and Counseling 1995, 10(2),* 1–4.

Chapter 5. Secondary Traumatic Stress Reactions in AIDS Group Practitioners

1. Eye Movement Desensitization is a procedure that requires the traumatized person to generate the image of the trauma in the mind while experiencing and verbalizing the associated physiological and emotional states. While concentrating on these states the trauma survivor follows with the eyes the therapist's finger, which is moved very rapidly side to side, ten to twenty times, eliciting from the survivor rhythmic bilateral saccadic eye movement. This procedure repeated subsequently with a range of trauma survivors has demonstrated positive outcomes (Marquis, 1991; Vaughan, Wiese, Gold, and Tarrier, 1994; Young, 1995; Wolpe and Abrams, 1991). To date, the literature substantiates the positive effects of this procedure, although it is the focus of continued negative commentary (Herbert and Mueser, 1992; Melter and Michelson, 1993). It appears that this procedure has the capacity to desensitize a highly traumatic memory within a short period of time (one session) without intense and prolonged anxiety, and can produce a cognitive restructuring that might as well address some aspects of the cognitive changes brought on by vicarious traumatization. For a complete conceptualization of this intervention, see F. Schapiro (1995), *Eye Movement Desensitization and Reprocessing: Basic Principle Protocols and Procedure.* Guilford Press: New York.

References

ACT-UP/NY. (1990). *Women, AIDS & activism*. Boston: South End Press.

ACT-UP/NY (1991). *ACT-UP New York: Capsule history*. New York: ACT-UP.

Adams, J. (1979). Mutual-help groups: Enhancing the coping ability of onocology clients. *Cancer Nursing*, 95–98.

Adelson, M. (1994). Clinical supervision of therapists with difficult-to-treat patients. *Bulletin of the Menninger Clinic*, *59*, 32–52.

Adler, G. (1972). Helplessness in the helpers. *British Journal of Medical Psychology*, *45*, 315–26.

Adler, G. (1984). Special problems for the therapist. *Journal of Psychiatry in Medicine*, *14(2)*, 91–98.

Alpher, V., & Kobos, J. (1988). Cotherapy in psychodynamic group psychotherapy: An approach to training. *Group*, *12(3)*, 125–44.

Altman, D. (1986). *AIDS in the mind of America*. New York: Anchor Press.

Amelio, R. (1993). An AIDS bereavement support group: One model of intervention in a time of crisis. *Social Work with Groups*, *16(1–2)*, 43–54.

American Psychiatric Association. (1980). *Diagnostic and statistical manual of mental disorders*. Washington, D.C.: American Psychiatric Association.

American Psychiatric Association. (1994). *Diagnostic and statistical manual of mental disorders*. Washington, D.C.: American Psychiatric Association.

Anderson, D., & Shaw, S. (1994). Starting support groups for families and partners of people with HIV/AIDS in a rural setting. *Social Work*, *39(1)*, 135–38.

Anthony, J. (1971). The history of group psychotherapy. In H. Kaplan

References

& B. Sadock (Eds.). *Comprehensive group psychotherapy* (pp. 4–31). Baltimore: Williams & Wilkins.

Appelbaum, P., & Greer, A. (1993). Confidentiality in group therapy. *Hospital and Community Psychiatry, 44(4)*, 311–12.

Assagioli, R. (1965). *Psychosytheis*. New York: Viking.

Assagioli, R. (1980). *The act of will*. New York: Penguin.

Barnes, P.F., & Barrows, S.A. (1993). Tuberculosis in the 1990s. *Annals of Internal Medicine, 119(5)*, 400–410.

Battin, M. (1994). Going early, going late: The rationality of decisions about suicide and AIDS. *Journal of Medicine and Philosophy, 19*, 571–94.

Baum, A., O'Keeffe, M., & Davidson, L. (1990). Acute stressors and chronic response: The case of traumatic stress. *Journal of Applied Social Psychology, 20(20)*, 1643–54.

Becker, E. (1973). *The denial of death*. New York: Free Press.

Beckerman, N.L. (1995). Suicide in relation to AIDS. *Death Studies, 19*, 223–34.

Beckett, A., & Kassel, P. (1994). Neuropsychiatric dysfunction: Impact on psychotherapy with HIV-infected gay men. In S. Cadwell, R. Burnham, & M. Forstein (Eds.). *Therapists on the front line: Psychotherapy with gay men in the age of AIDS* (pp. 147–62). Washington, D.C.: American Psychiatric Press.

Beckett, A., & Rutan, J.S. (1990). Treating persons with ARC and AIDS in psychotherapy. *International Journal of Group Psychotherapy, 40*, 19–29.

Belenky, M., Clinchy, B., Goldberger, N., & Tarule, J. (1986). *Women's ways of knowing: The development of self, voice, and mind*. New York: Basic Books.

Beltangady, M. (1988). The risk of suicide in persons with AIDS. *Journal of the American Medical Association, 260(1)*, 29.

Bennett, L., Kelaher, M., & Ross, M. (1994a). Quality of life in health care professionals: Burnout and its associated factors in HIV/AIDS related care. *Psychology and Health, 9(4)*, 273–83.

Bennett, L., Kelaher, M., & Ross, M. (1994b). The impact of working with HIV/AIDS on health care professionals: Development of the AIDS impact scale. *Psychology and Health, 9(3)*, 221–32.

Bernstein, G., & Klein, R. (1995). Countertransference issues in group psychotherapy with HIV-positive and AIDS patients. *International Journal of Group Psychotherapy, 45(1)*, 91–101.

Bibring, E. (1953). The mechanisms of depression. In P. Greenacre

181

References

(Ed.). *Affective disorders: Psycho-analytic contribution to their study* (pp. 13–48). New York: International Press.

Biller, R., & Rice, S. (1990). Experiencing multiple loss of persons with AIDS: Grief and bereavement issues. *Health & Social Work, 15*, 283–90.

Blechner, M. (1993). Psychoanalysis and HIV disease. *Contemporary Psychoanalysis, 29*, 61–80.

Block, S. (1961). Multi-leadership as a teaching and therapeutic tool in group practice. *Comprehensive Psychiatry, 2*, 211–18.

Borghi, L. (1978). Group psychotherapy experience with special reference to transference and countertransference with the group and between co-therapists. *Group Analysis, 11*, 247–58.

Bowlby, J. (1969). *Attachment and Loss (Vol. I, Separation: anxiety and anger)*. New York: Basic Books.

Bowlby, J. (1973). *Attachment and loss (Vol. II, Separation: anxiety and anger)*. New York: Basic Books.

Boyd, C. (1993). The antecedents of women's crack cocaine abuse: Family substance abuse, sexual abuse, depression and illicit drug use. *Journal of Substance Abuse Treatment, 10*, 433–38.

Boykin, F. (1991). The AIDS crises and gay male survivor guilt. *Smith Studies in Social Work, 61(3)*, 247–59.

Brayborg, T., & Marks, M. (1973). Transference variation evoked by racial differences in cotherapists. In J.A. Goodman (Ed.). *Dynamics of racism in social work practice* (pp. 214–20). Washington, D.C.: National Association of Social Workers.

Brende, J., & Goldsmith, R. (1991). Post-traumatic stress disorder in families. *Journal of Contemporary Psychotherapy, 21(2)*, 115–24.

Brett, E., & Mangine, W. (1985). Imagery and combat stress in Vietnam veterans. *Journal of Nervous and Mental Diseases, 173*, 309–11.

Brett, E., & Ostroff, R. (1985). Imagery and post-traumatic stress disorder: An overview. *American Journal of Psychiatry, 142(4)*, 417–24.

Brettle, R., & Lean, C. (1991). The natural history of HIV and AIDS in women. *AIDS, 5*, 1283–92.

Brody, H. (1992). Assisted death: A compassionate response to a medical failure. *New England Journal of Medicine, 327*, 1384–88.

Buck, B. (1991). Support groups for hospitalized AIDS patients. *AIDS Patient Care, 2*, 255–58.

Buelow, G. (1994). A suicide in group: A case of functional realignment. *International Journal of Group Psychotherapy, 44*, 153–68.

182

References

Buie, J. (1989). Legal limits, loose lips threaten group privacy. *APA Monitor*, November 23, 24.

Burgress, A., & Holmstrom, L. (1974). Rape trauma syndrome. *American Journal of Psychiatry, 131*, 981–86.

Burgress, A., & Holstrom, L. (1979). Adaptive strategies and recovery from rape. *American Journal of Psychiatry, 136*, 1278–82.

Burke, J., Coddington, D., Bakeman, R., & Clance, P. (1994). Inclusion and exclusion in HIV support groups. *Journal of Gay and Lesbian Psychotherapy, 2(2)*, 121–30.

Burnham, R. (1994). Trauma revisited: HIV and AIDS gay male survivors of early sexual abuse. In S. Cadwell, R. Burnham, & M. Forstein (Eds.). *Therapists on the front line: Psychotherapy with gay men in the age of AIDS* (pp. 379–404). Washington, D.C.: American Psychiatric Press.

Cadwell, S. (1994a). Twice removed: The stigma suffered by gay men with AIDS. In S. Cadwell, R. Burnham, & M. Forstein (Eds.). *Therapists on the front line: Psychotherapy with gay men in the age of AIDS* (pp. 3–24). Washington, D.C.: American Psychiatric Press.

Cadwell, S. (1994b). Empathic challenges for gay male therapists working with HIV infected gay men. In S. Cadwell, R. Burnham, & M. Forstein (Eds.). *Therapists on the front line: Psychotherapy with gay men in the age of AIDS* (pp. 475–96) Washington, D.C.: American Psychiatric Press.

Cadwell, S., Burnham, R., & Forstein, M. (1994). *Therapists on the front line: Psychotherapy with gay men in the age of AIDS*. Washington, D.C.: American Psychiatric Press.

California Supreme Court. (1976). Tarasoff v. The Regents of the University of California. 17 Cal. 3d 425, 551 P.2d 334. *Cal 3d, 425.*

Caligor, L. (1981). Parallel and reciprocal processes in psychoanalytic supervision. *Contemporary Psychoanalysis, 17*, 1–27.

Caplan, G. (1974). *Support systems and community mental health.* New York: Behavioral Publications.

Caputo, L. (1985). Dual diagnosis: AIDS and addictions. *Social Work, 30*, 361–64.

Caschetta, M.B., & Franke-Ruta, G. (Eds). (1992). Special edition women's treatment issues. *GMHC Treatment News, 6(7)* 1–27.

Cassese, J. (1993). The invisible bridge: Child sex abuse and the risk of HIV infection in adulthood. *Siecus Report, 21(4)*, 1–7.

Castro, K., Valdiserri, O., & Curran, J. (1992). Perspective on

References

HIV/AIDS epidemiology and prevention from the Eighth International Conference on AIDS. *American Journal of Public Health,* *82,* 1465–70.

Catherall, D.R. (1995). Preventing institutional secondary traumatic stress disorder. In C.R. Figley (Ed.). *Compassion fatigue: Coping with secondary traumatic stress disorder in those who treat the traumatized* (pp. 232–57). New York: Brunner/Mazel.

Cerney, M. (1985). Imaging and grief work. *Psychotherapy, 2(1),* 35–44.

Cherus, L., & Livingston, P. (1993). Clinical supervision: Its role in "containing" countertransference responses to a filicidal patient. *Clinical Social Work Journal 2(4),* 349–64.

Chessick, R.D. (1978). The sad soul of the psychiatrist. *Bulletin of the Menninger Clinic, 42,* 1–9.

Christensen, K. (1992). Prison issues and HIV: Introduction. In ACT UP/NY WOMEN and AIDS Book Group (Ed.). *Women, AIDS & activism* (pp. 139–42). Boston: South End Press.

Cho, C., & Cassidy, D. (1994). Parallel processes for workers and their clients in chronic bereavement resulting from HIV. *Death Studies, 18,* 273–92.

Chu, S., Buehler, T., & Berkelman, R. (1990). Impact of the human immunodeficiency virus epidemic in mortality in women of reproductive age in the United States. *Journal of the American Medical Association, 264,* 225–26.

Clever, L.H., & LeGuyader, V. (1995). Infectious risks for health care workers. *Annual Review of Public Health, 16,* 141–64.

Coates, T.J., Stall, R.A., & Mandel, J.S. (1987). AIDS: A psychosocial research agenda. *Archives of Behavioral Medicine, 9,* 21–28.

Cobb, S. (1976). Social support as a moderator of life. *Psychosomatic Medicine, 38,* 300–314.

Cochran, S., & Mays, V. (1989). Women and AIDS-related concerns: Roles for psychologists in helping the worried well. *American Psychologist, 44,* 529–38.

Cohen, S. (1988). Psychosocial models of the role of social support in the etiology of physical disease. *Health Psychology, 7,* 269–97.

Cooper, L. (1976). Co-therapy relationships in groups. *Small Group Behavior, 7,* 473–98.

Cooper, L., & Gustafson, J. (1985). Supervision in a group: An application of group therapy. *Clinical Supervisor, 3(2),* 7–25.

References

Corazzini, J., & Heppner, P. (1982). Client-therapist preparation for group therapy: Expanding the diagnostic interview. *Small Group Behavior, 13(2)*, 219–36.

Cote, T.R., Biggar, R., & Dannenberg, A. (1992). Risk of suicide among persons with AIDS. *Journal of the American Medical Association, 268(15)*, 2066–68.

Couch, D. (1995). Four steps for conducting a pregroup screening interview. *Journal for Specialists in Group Work, 20(1)*, 18–25.

Counselman, F., & Gumpert, P. (1993). Psychotherapy supervision in small leader-led groups. *Group, 17(1)*, 25–32.

Dane, B. (1994). Helping health professionals overcome grief associated with caring for AIDS patients. In W. Odets & M. Shernoff (Eds.). *The second decade of AIDS: A mental health practice handbook* (pp. 275–92). New York: Hatherleigh Press.

Danieli, Y. (1984). Psychotherapists' participation in the conspiracy of silence about the Holocaust. *Psychoanalytic Psychology, 1(1)*, 23–42.

Danieli, Y. (1985). The treatment and prevention of long-term effects and intergenerational transmission of victimization: A lesson from Holocaust survivors. In C.R. Figley (Ed.). *Trauma and its wake: The study and treatment of post-traumatic stress disorder* (pp. 295–98). New York: Brunner/Mazel.

Daniolos, P. (1994). House calls: A support group for individuals with AIDS in a community residential setting. *International Journal of Group Psychotherapy, 44(2)*, 133–52.

Daste, B. (1990). Important considerations in group work with cancer patients. *Social Work with Groups, 13(2)*, 69–81.

Davis, K., & Meara, N. (1982). So you think it is a secret. *Journal for Specialists in Group Work, 7*, 149–53.

Dean, R.G. (1995). Stories of AIDS: The use of narrative as an approach to understanding in an AIDS support group. *Clinical Social Work Journal, 23(3)*, 287–304.

Demarest, E., & Teicher, A. (1954). Transference in group psychotherapy: Its use by co-therapists of opposite sexes. *Psychiatry, 17*, 187–202.

Denenberg, R. (1990). Unique aspects of HIV infection in women. In The ACT/UP/NY Women & AIDS book group (Ed.). *Women, AIDS & activism* (2d ed.) (pp. 31–44). Boston: South End Press.

Denenberg, R. (1994). Special concerns of women with HIV and AIDS. In W. Odelts & M. Shernoff (Eds.). *The second decade of*

References

AIDS: A mental health practice handbook (pp. 115–36). New York: Hatherleigh Press.

Dhooper, S.S., & Royse, D.S. (1989). Rural attitudes about AIDS: A statewide survey. *Human Services in the Rural Environment, 13,* 17–22.

Dick, B., Lesser, K., & Whiteside, J. (1980). A developmental framework for cotherapy. *International Journal of Group Psychotherapy, 30(3),* 273–85.

Doehrman, M.J. (1976). Parallel process in supervision and psychotherapy. *Bulletin of the Meninger Clinic, 40,* 9–104.

Doka, K.J. (1987). Silent sorrow: Grief and the loss of significant others. *Death Studies, 11(6),* 455–69.

Drucker, A. (1992) HIV-related challenges for rural therapists. *FOCUS: A guide to AIDS Research and Counseling 7(5),* 1–4.

Dunkel, J., & Hatfield, S. (1986). Countertransference issues in working with persons with AIDS. *Social Work, 31(2),* 114–17.

Eissler, K. (1955). *The psychiatrist and the dying patient.* New York: International Universities Press.

El-Mallakh, P.L., & El-Mallakh, R.S. (1989). Group psychotherapy for AIDS patients. *AIDS Patient Care, 3,* 18–20.

Erickson, S. (1990). Counseling the irresponsible AIDS client: Guidelines for decision making. *Journal of Counseling and Development, 68,* 454–55.

Erickson, S. (1993). Ethics and confidentiality in AIDS counseling: A professional dilemma. *Journal of Mental Health Counseling, 15(2),* 118–31.

Ettin, M. (1988). "By the crowd they have been broken, by the crowd they shall be healed": The advent of group psychotherapy. *International Journal of Group Psychotherapy, 38(2),* 139–67.

Farber, E. (1994). Psychotherapy with HIV and AIDS patients: The phenomenon of helplessness in therapists. *Psychotherapy, 31,* 715–24.

Farberow, N.L. (1992). The Los Angeles Survivor-After-Suicide Program: An evaluation. *Crisis, 13,* 23–34.

Fella, P., Rivera, P., Sepdowitz, K., Hale, M., & Ramos, Z. (1992). Dramatic increase in cases of three-drug resistant TB in an urban community hospital. *International Conference on AIDS, 8(2)B99,* 19–24.

Ferenzci, S. (1924). On forced fantasies. In J. Richman (Ed.). *Further*

References

contributions to the theory and technique of psychoanalysis (pp. 68–77). New York: Brunner/Mazel.

Ferlic, M., Goldman, A.J., & Kennedy, B.J. (1979). Group counseling in adult patients with advanced cancer. *Cancer, 43*, 760–66.

Field, H., & Shore, M. (1992). Living and dying with AIDS: Report of a three-year psychotherapy group. *Group, 16(3),* 156–64.

Figley, C. (1986). Traumatic stress: The role of the family and social support system. In C. Figley (Ed.). *Trauma and its wake* (pp. 39–58). New York: Brunner/Mazel.

Figley, C. (1987). Post-traumatic therapy and victims of violence. In C. Figely (Ed.). *Post-traumatic therapy and victims of violence* (pp. 3–24). New York: Brunner/Mazel.

Figely, C. (1995). *Compassion fatigue: Coping with secondary traumatic stress disorder in those who treat the traumatized.* New York: Brunner/Mazel.

Figley, C. (1983). Catastrophe: An overview of family reactions. In C. Figley & H.E. McCubkin (Eds.). *Stress and the family: Volume 2, Coping with catastrophe* (pp. 3–20). New York: Brunner/Mazel.

Fishman, J. (1995). Countertransference, the therapeutic frame and AIDS: One psychotherapist's response. In S. Cadwell, R. Burnham, & M. Forstein (Eds.). *Therapists on the front line: Psychotherapy with gay men in the age of AIDS* (pp. 497–516). Washington, D.C.: American Psychiatric Press.

Flannery, R. (1990). Social support and psychological trauma: A methodological review. *Journal of Traumatic Stress, 3(4),* 593–610.

Flannery, R., Fulton, P., Tausch, J., & Deloffi, A. (1991). A program to help staff cope with psychological sequelae of assaults by patients. *Hospital & Community Psychiatry, 42(9),* 935–38.

Flannery, R., & Harvey, M. (1991). Psychological trauma and learned helplessness: Seligman's paradigm reconsidered. *Psychotherapy, 28(2),* 374–78.

Flannery, R. (1990). *Becoming stress resistant.* New York: Continuum.

Flapan, D., & Fenchel, G.H. (1984). Countertransference in group psychotherapy. *Group, 8(3),* 17–29.

Forstein, M. (1994). Suicidality and HIV in gay men. In S. Cadwell, R. Burnham, & M. Forstein (Eds.). *Therapists on the front line: Psychotherapy with gay men in the age of AIDS* (pp. 111–46). Washington, D.C.: American Psychiatric Press.

References

Frances, D., & Dugo, J. (1985). Pretherapy orientation as preparation for open psychotherapy group. *Psychotherapy, 22(2),* 256–61.

Frank, G. (1953). The literature on countertransference: A survey. *International Journal of Group Psychotherapy, 3,* 441–80.

Freud, S. (1910). The future prospects of psycho-analytic therapy. *Standard Edition, 11,* 139–51.

Freud, S. (1920). Beyond the pleasure principle. *Standard Edition,* 18, 3–64. London: Hogarth Press.

Freudenberger, H.J. (1974). Staff burn-out. *Journal of Social Issues, 30(1),* 159–65.

Friedland, G. (1989). Clinical care in the AIDS epidemic. *Daedalus, 118,* 59–83.

Frierson, R., & Lippman, S. (1988). Suicide and AIDS. *Psychosomatics, 29,* 226–31.

Frost, J. (1993). Group psychotherapy with HIV Positive and AIDS patients. In A. Alonso & H. Swiller (Eds.). *Group psychotherapy in clinical practice* (pp. 255–70). Washington, D.C.: American Psychiatric Press.

Gabriel, M. (1991). Group therapists' countertransference reactions to multiple deaths from AIDS. *Clinical Social Work Journal, 19(3),* 279–91.

Gabriel, M. (1993). The cotherapy relationship: Special issues and problems in AIDS therapy groups. *Group, 17(1),* 33–42.

Gabriel, M. (1994). Group therapists and AIDS groups: An exploration of traumatic stress reactions. *Group, 17(3),* 167–76.

Gallo, R.C., & Montagnier, L. (1988). AIDS in 1988. *Scientific American, 4,* 40–51.

Gambe, R., & Getzel, G. (1989). Group work with gay men with AIDS. *Social Casework, 70,* 172–88.

Gans, R. (1957). The use of group co-therapists in the teaching of psychotherapy. *American Journal of Psychotherapy, 11,* 618–25.

Gans, R. (1962). Group co-therapists and the therapeutic situation: A critical evaluation. *International Journal of Group Psychotherapy, 19(3),* 366–81.

Garside, B. (1993). Physicians' mutual AID groups: A response to AIDS related burnout. *Health and Social Work, 18(4),* 259–67.

Germain, C., & Gitterman, A. (1980). *The life model of social work practice.* New York: Columbia University Press.

References

Gerson, B.P., & Carlier, I.V. (1992). Posttraumatic stress disorder: The history of the recent concept. *British Journal of Psychiatry, 16,* 742–44.

Getzel, G. (1994). No one is alone: Groups during the AIDS pandemic. In A. Gitterman & L. Shulman (Eds.). *Mutual aid, groups vulnerable populations, and the life cycle* (pp. 185–98). New York: Columbia University Press.

Getzel, G., & Mahony, K. (1990). Confronting human finitude: Group work with people with AIDS. *Journal of Gay and Lesbian Psychotherapy, 1,* 105–20.

Gibson, C. (1991). A concept analysis of empowerment. *Journal of Advanced Nursing, 16,* 354–61.

Gilden, D. (1995). Treatment briefs. *GMHC Treatment Issues, 9(4),* 6.

Gilden, D. (1996). Let there be drugs. *GMHC Treatment Issues 10(2),* 1 & 13.

Gilligan, C. (1982). *In a different voice: Women's conceptions of self and of morality.* New York: Garland.

Gitterman, A. (1989). Building mutual support in groups. *Social Work with Groups, 12(2),* 5–21.

Glass, R.M. (1988). AIDS and suicide. *Journal of the American Medical Association, 259,* 1369–70.

Goldman, S. (1989). Bearing the unbearable: The psychological impact of AIDS. In J. Offerman-Zuckerman (Ed.). *Gender in transition: A new frontier* (pp. 263–74). New York: Plenum.

Grand, H. (1982). Unique transference elements in co-therapy groups. In L. Wolberg & M. Aronson (Eds.). *Group and family therapy 1982* (pp. 109–18). New York: Brunner/Mazel.

Gray, E., & Harding, A. (1988). Confidentiality limits with clients who have the AIDS virus. *Journal of Counseling and Development, 66,* 219–23.

Green, B. (1990). Defining trauma: Terminology and generic stressor dimensions. *Journal of Applied Social Psychology, 20(20),* 1632–42.

Green, B.L., Wilson, J.P., & Lindy, J.D. (1985). Conceptualizing posttraumatic stress disorder: A psychosocial framework. In C.R. Figley (Ed.). *Trauma and its wake.* New York: Brunner/Mazel.

Gregory, J., & McConnell, S. (1986). Ethical issues with psychotherapy in group contexts. *Psychotherapy in Private Practice, 4,* 51–62.

Grigsby, J. (1987). The use of imagery in the treatment of postraumatic stress disorder. *Journal of Nervous & Mental Diseases, 175(1),* 55–59.

References

Grossman, A., & Silverstein, C. (1993). Facilitating support groups for professionals working with people with AIDS. *Social Work, 38(2),* 141–51.

Grotjahn, M. (1953). Special aspects of countertransference in analytic group psychotherapy. *International Journal of Group Psychotherapy, 3,* 407–16.

Gunter, M. (1994). Countertransference issues in staff caregivers who work to rehabilitate catastrophic injury survivors. *American Journal of Psychotherapy, 48(2),* 208–20.

Gutierrez, L. (1990). Working with women of color: An empowerment perspective. *Social Work, 35(3),* 149–53.

Haas, A., & Hendin, H. (1986). What is the role of traumatic imagery. *American Journal of Psychiatry, 143(1),* 124.

Hadden, S. (1953). Countertransference in the group. *International Journal of Group Psychotherapy, 3,* 417–23.

Halperin, D. (1989). Countertransference and group psychotherapy: The role of supervision. In D. Halperin (Ed.). *Group psychodynamics: New paradigms and new perspectives* (pp. 62–75). Chicago: Year Book Medical Publishers.

Haney, P. (1988). Providing empowerment to the person with AIDS. *Social Work, 33(3),* 251–56.

Hartman, E.R., & Jackson, H. (1994). Rape and the phenomenon of countertransference. In J.P. Wilson & J.L. Lindy (Eds.). *Countertransference in the treatment of PTSD* (pp. 206–44). New York: Guilford Press.

Heideggar, M. (1962). *Being and time.* New York: Harper and Row.

Heimann, P. (1950). On countertransference. *International Journal of Psychoanalysis, 31,* 81–84.

Herbert, J.D., & Mueser, K.T. (1992). Eye movement desensitization: A critique of the evidence. *Journal of Behavioral Therapy and Experimental Psychiatry, 23,* 167–74.

Herek, G., & Glunt, E. (1988). An epidemic of stigma: Public reactions to AIDS. *American Psychologist, 43(11),* 198–203.

Herman, J. (1992). *Trauma and recovery.* New York: Basic Books.

Herman, J., & Hirschman, L. (1977). Father-daughter incest. *Signs, 2(4),* 735–56.

Hirsch, D.A., & Enlow, R.W. (1984). The effects of the acquired immune deficiency syndrome on gay life style and the gay individual. *Annals of New York Academy of Science, 437,* 273–82.

References

Honey, E. (1988). AIDS and the inner city: Critical issues. *Social Casework, 69(6)*, 365–70.

Hopewell, P.C. (1992). Impact of human immunodeficiency virus infection on the epidemiology, clinical features, management and control of tuberculosis. *Clinical Infectious Disease, 15(3)*, 540–47.

Hora, T. (1957). Contribution to the phenomenology of the supervisory process. *American Journal of Psychotherapy, 11*, 769–73.

Horowitz, M.J. (1970). *Image formation and cognition.* New York: Appleton-Century-Crofts.

Horowitz, M.J. (1976). *Stress response syndromes.* New York: Jason Aronson.

Horowitz, M.J. (1979). *States of mind.* New York: Plenum.

Houseman, C., & Pheifer, W. (1988). Potential for unresolved grief in survivors of persons with AIDS. *Archives of Psychiatric Nursing, 2(5)*, 296–301.

Hughes, R., & Friedman, A. (1994). AIDS-related ethical and legal issues for mental health. *Journal of Mental Health Counseling, 16(4)*, 443–58.

Hunter, N. (1995). Complications of gender: Women, AIDS and the law. In B. Schneider & N. Stoller (Eds.). *Women resisting AIDS: Feminist strategies of empowerment* (pp. 32–56). Philadephia: Temple University Press.

Hyland, J.M., Pruyser, H., Novotny, E., & Coyne, L. (1984). The impact of the death of a group member in a group of breast cancer patients. *International Journal of Group Psychotherapy, 34(4)*, 617–26.

Janoff-Bulman, R. (1985). The aftermath of victimization: Rebuilding shattered assumptions. In C. Figley (Ed.). *Trauma and its wake: The study of treatment of post-traumatic stress* (pp. 15–35). New York: Brunner/Mazel.

Janoff-Bulman, R. (1992). *Shattered asumptions.: Towards a new psychology of trauma.* New York: Basic Books.

Jemmott, J.B., & Locke, S.E. (1984). Psychological factors, immunological mediation and human susceptibility to infectious disease. *Psychological Bulletin, 95*, 78–108.

Joinson, C. (1992). Coping with compassion fatigue. *Nursing, 22(4)*, 116–22.

Jones, A., & Crandall, R. (1985). Preparing newcomers to enhance assimilation into groups. *Small Group Behavior, 16*, 31–57.

Jordan, J., Kaplan, A., Miller, J., Stiver, I, & Surrey, J. (1991). *Women's growth in connection: Writings from the Stone Center.* New York, Guilford Press.

Jung, C.G. (1928). *The archetypes and the collective unconscious.* New York: Pantheon.

Kabat-Zinn, J. (1990). *Full catastrophe living: Using the wisdom of your body and mind to face stress, pain and illness.* New York: Dekta Books.

Kain, C. (1988). To breach or not to breach: Is that the question? *Journal of Counseling and Development, 66,* 224–25.

Kain, C.D. (1989). *No longer immune: A counselor's guide to AIDS.* Alexandria: American Association for Counseling and Development.

Kane-Cavaiola, C., & Rullo-Cooney, M.A. (1991). Addicted women: Their families' effect on treatment outcome. *Journal of Chemical Dependency Treatment,* 111–19.

Kapila, R., & Kloser, P. (1988). Women and AIDS: An overview. *Medical Aspects of Human Sexuality, 22,* 92–103.

Kaplan, B.H., Cassel, J.C., & Gore, S. (1979). Social support and health. *Medical Care, 15,* 47–58.

Karakashian, M. (1994). Countertransference issues in crisis work with natural disasters. *Psychotherapy, 31(2),* 334–41.

Kardiner, A., & Spiegel, H. (1947). *War stress and neurotic illness.* New York: International Universities Press.

Kassel, P.E. (1990). Psychological and neurological dimensions of HIV illness. In J.A. Mukand (Ed.). *AIDS and rehabilitation medicine.* New York: McGraw Hill.

Kastenbaum, R.A., & Aisenberg, R. (1972). *The psychology of death.* New York: Springer.

Kauffman, E., Dore, M., & Nelson-Zlupko, L. (1995). The role of women's therapy groups in the treatment of chemical dependence. *American Journal of Orthopsychiatry, 65(3),* 355–63.

Keane, T.M., Scott, W.O., Chavoya, G.A., Lamparski, D.M., & Fairbanks, A. (1985). Social support in Vietnam veterans with posttraumatic stress disorder: An empirical analysis. *Journal of Consulting and Clinical Psychology, 53(1),* 95–102.

Keane, T.M., Caddell, J.M., & Taylor, K.L. (1988). Mississippi Scale for combat-related posttraumatic stress disorder. *Journal of Consulting and Clinical Psychology, 56,* 85–90.

Keane, T.M., Gerardi, R., Lyons, J., & Wolfe, J. (1988). The interrelationship of substance abuse and posttraumatic stress: Epidemiological and clinical considerations. *Recent Developments in Alcoholism, 6*, 27–48.

Kearney, M. (1984). Confidentiality in group psychotherapy. *Psychotherapy in Private Practice, 2*, 19–20.

Kelly, J., & Sykes, P. (1989). Helping the helpers: A support group for family members of persons with AIDS. *Social Work, 34(3)*, 239–42.

Kemeny, M.E., Weiner, H., Taylor, S.E., Schneider, S., Visscher, B., & Fahey, J.L. (1994). Repeated bereavement, depressed mood and immune parameter in HIV seropositive and seronegative gay men. *Health Psychology, 13(1)*, 14–24.

Kermani, E., & Weiss, B. (1989). AIDS and confidentiality: Legal concept and its application in psychotherapy. *American Journal of Psychotherapy, 43*, 25–28.

Kernberg, O. (1964). Notes on countertransference. *Journal of the American Psychoanalytic Association, 13*, 38–50.

Kevorkian, J. (1991). *Prescription medicine: The goodness of planned death.* Buffalo: Prometheus Books.

Kibel, H. (1973). A group member's suicide: Treating collective trauma. *International Journal of Group Psychotherapy, 23*, 43–53.

Kiecolt-Glaser, J.K., & Glaser, R. (1986). Psychosocial moderators of immune function. *Annals of Behavioral Medicine, 9*, 3–10.

Kiecolt-Glaser, J.K., & Glaser, R. (1995). Psychoneuroimmunology and health consequences: Data and shared mechanisms. *Psychosomatic Medicine, 57(3)*, 269–79.

Kilborn, R. (1994). Alarming trend among workers: Surveys find clusters of TB cases. *New York Times, January 23, 1994*, 1, 16.

Kinzie, J.D., & Boehnlein, J. (1993). Psychotherapy of the victims of massive violence: Countertransference and ethical issues. *American Journal of Psychotherapy, 47(1)*, 90–102.

Kirtley, D. (1969). Reactions of a psychotherapy group to ambiguous circumstances surrounding the death of a group member. *International Journal of Group Psychotherapy, 33(2)*, 195–99.

Klonoff, E.A., & Ewers, D. (1990). Care of AIDS patients as a source of stress to nursing staff. *AIDS Education and Prevention, 2(4)*, 338–48.

Knapp, S., & VandeCreek, L. (1990). Application of the duty to protect HIV-positive patients. *Professional Psychology: Research and Practice, 21(3)*, 161–66.

References

Koller, P., Marmar, C.R., & Kanas, N. (1992). Psychodynamic group treatment of post-traumatic stress disorder in Vietnam veterans. *International Journal of Group Psychotherapy, 42,* 224–46.

Krystal, H. (1968). *Massive trauma.* New York: International Universities Press.

Krystal, H. (1978). Trauma and affects. *Psychoanalytic Study of the Child, 33,* 81–116.

Lamb, D.H., Clark, C., Drumheller, P., Frizzell, K., & Surrey, L. (1989). Appling Tarasoff to AIDS-related psychotherapy issues. *Professional Psychology: Research and Practice, 20(1),* 37–43.

Lee, J., & Swenson, C. (1994). The concept of mutual aid. In A. Gitterman & L. Shulman (Eds.). *Mutual aid, groups vulnerable populations and the life cycle* (pp. 413–30). New York: Columbia University Press.

Lenihan, M. (1995). Morning support group: Use of a triweekly support group in outpatient treatment of chemical dependence. *Social Work, 40,* 127–31.

Lennon, M.D., Martin, J.L., & Dean, L. (1990). The influence of social support on AIDS-related grief reactions among gay men. *Social Science and Medicine, 31(4),* 477–84.

Leszca, M., & Murphy, L. (1994). Supervision of group psychotherapy. In Anonymous (Ed.). *Clinical perspectives on psychotherapy supervision* (pp. 99–120). Washington, D.C.: American Psychiatric Press.

Levine, C. (1993). *A death in the family: Orphans of the HIV epidemic.* New York: United Hospital Fund.

Levy, R.M., Bredesen, D.E., & Rosenblum, M.L. (1985). Neurological manifestations of the acquired immunodeficiency syndrome: Experience at UCSF and review of literature. *Journal of Neurosurgery, 62,* 475–95.

Lifton, R.J. (1968). *Death in life: Survivors of Hiroshima.* New York: Random House.

Lifton, R.J. (1970). *History and human survival; essays on the young and old, survivors and the dead, peace, war and on contemporary psychohistory.* New York: Random House.

Lifton, R.J. (1973). *Home from the war: Vietnam veterans neither victims nor executioners.* New York: Simon & Schuster.

Lifton, R.J. (1976). The human meaning of total disaster: The Buffalo Creek experience. *Psychiatry, 39,* 1–17.

Lifton, R.J. (1979). *The broken connection: On death and the continuity of life*. New York: Basic Books.

Lifton, R.J. (1982). The psychology of the survivor and the death imprint. *Psychiatric Annals, 12*, 1011–20.

Lindemann, E. (1944). Symptomatology and management of acute grief. *American Journal of Psychiatry, 101*, 141–48.

Lindy, J.D. (1988). *Vietnam: A casebook*. New York: Brunner/Mazel.

Little, M. (1951). Countertransference and the patient's response to it. *International Journal of Psychoanalysis, 32*, 32–40.

Loeser, L.H., & Bry, T. (1953). The position of the group therapist in transference and countertransference: An experimental study. *International Journal of Group Psychotherapy, 3*, 389–406.

Lonetto, R., & Templer, D. (1986). *Death anxiety*. Washington, D.C.: Hemisphere.

Lopes, S. (1994). *Living with AIDS: A photographic journal*. New York: Little, Brown.

Lothstein, L.M. (1978). The group psychotherapy dropout phenomenon revisited. *Journal of Psychiatry, 135*, 1492–95.

Lunn, S., Skydsbjerg, M., & Schulsinger, H. (1991). A prelminary report on the neuropsychologic sequelae of human immunodeficiency virus. *Archives of General Psychiatry, 48*, 139–42.

Macks, J. (1988). Women and AIDS: Countertransference issues. *Social Casework, 69*, 471–81.

MacLennan, B. (1965). Co-therapy. *International Journal of Group Psychotherapy, 15*, 154–66.

Marquis, J.N. (1991). A report on seventy-eight cases treated by eye movement desensitization. *Journal of Behavior Therapy and Experimental Psychiatry, 22*, 187–92.

Martin, H.P. (1991). The coming out process for homosexuals. *Hospital Community Psychiatry, 42*, 158–62.

Martin, J.L. (1988). Psychological consequences of AIDS related bereavement among gay men. *Journal of Counseling and Clinical Psychology, 56(6)*, 856–62.

Martin, M.L., & Henry-Feeny, J. (1989). Clinical services to people with AIDS: The parallel nature of the client and worker processes. *Clinical Social Work Journal, 17*, 337–48.

Marzuk, P., Tierney, H., Tardiff, K., Gross, E., Morgan, E., Hsu, M., & Mann, J. (1988). Increased risk of suicide in persons with AIDS. *Journal of the American Medical Association, 259(9)*, 1333–37.

References

Maslach, C. (1976). Burned out. *Human Behavior, 5*, 16–22.

Maslach, C. (1982). *Burnout: The cost of caring.* Englewood Cliffs, N.J.: Prentice-Hall.

Maslach, C., & Jackson, S. (1982). Burnout in health professionals: A social psychological analysis. In G. Sanders & J. Suls (Eds.). *Social psychology of health and illness* (pp. 227–51). Hillsdale, N. J.: Lawrence Erlbaum Associates.

Mayer, K., & Carpenter, C. (1992). Women and AIDS. *Scientific American, 266,* 118.

Mays, V., & Cockran, S. (1988). Issues in the perception of AIDS risk and risk education activities by black and Hispanic women. *American Psychologist, 43,* 949–57.

McFarlane, A.C. (1990). Vulnerability to post-traumatic stress disorder. In M.E. Wolf & A.D. Mosnaims (Eds.). *Post-traumatic stress disorder: Etiology, phenomenology and treatment* (pp. 2–21). Washington, D.C.: American Psychiatric Press.

McCallum, M., Piper, W., & Joyce, A. (1992). Dropping out from short-term group therapy. *Psychotherapy, 29,* 206–13.

McCann, I., & Pearlman, L. (1990a). Vicarious traumatization: A framework for understanding the psychological effects of working with victims. *Journal of Traumatic Stress, 3(1),* 131–49.

McCann, I., & Pearlman, L. (1990b). *Psychological trauma and the adult survivor.* New York: Brunner/Mazel.

McDougall, J. (1979). Primitive communication and the use of countertransference. In L. Epstein & A. Feiner (Eds.). *Countertransference: The therapist's contribution to the therapeutic situation* (pp. 267–303). New York: Aronson Press.

McElroy, L., & McElroy, R. (1991). Countertransference issues in the treatment of incest families. *Psychotherapy, 28(1),* 48–54.

McFarlane, A.C. (1992). The prevalence of posttraumatic stress disorder in the Vietnam generation: A multi-method, multi-source assessment of psychiatric disorder. *Journal of Traumatic Stress, 5,* 333–63.

McKegney, F.P., & O'Dowd, M.A. (1992). Suicidality and HIV. *American Journal of Psychiatry, 149,* 396–98.

McKusick, L. (1988). The impact of AIDS on practitioner and client: Notes for the therapeutic relationship. *American Psychologist, 43(11),* 935–40.

McWhirter, E. (1991). Empowerment in counseling. *Journal of Counseling and Development, 69(3),* 222–27.

References

Melter, J., & Michelson, L.K. (1993). Commentary: Theoretical clinical research and ethical constraints of the eye movement desensitization. *Journal of Traumatic Stress, 6,* 413–15.

Melton, G. (1988). Ethical and legal issues in AIDS-related practice. *American Psychologist, 43(11),* 941–47.

Mervin, M., & Smith-Kurtz, B. (1988). Healing of the whole person. In F.M. Ochberg (Ed.). *Post-traumatic therapy and victims of violence* (pp. 57–82). New York: Brunner/Mazel.

Miller, D., & Thelen, M. (1987). Confidentiality in psychotherapy: History, issues, and research. *Psychotherapy, 24(4),* 704–11.

Miller, J. (1988). *Connections, disconnections and violations.* Wellesley, Mass.: Stone Center.

Miller, J.B. (1986). *Toward a new psychology of women.* Boston: Beacon Press.

Miller, J.B., & Stiver, I. (1993). A relational approach to understanding women's lives and problems. *Psychiatric Annals, 23(8),* 424–31.

Mintz, E. (1963). Special values of co-therapists in group psychotherapy. *International Journal of Group Psychotherapy, 13(2),* 127–32.

Misbin, R. (1991). Physicians' aid in dying. *New England Journal of Medicine, 325,* 1307–10.

Molnos, A. (1990). *Our responses to a deadly virus: The group-analytic approach.* London: Karnac Books.

Momeyer, R. (1995). Does physician assisted suicide violate the integrity of medicine? *Journal of Medicine and Psychiatry, 20,* 13–24.

Morrison, C.F. (1989). AIDS: Ethical implications for psychological intervention. *Professional Psychology: Research and Practice, 20,* 166–74.

Moss, A.R. (1987). AIDS and intravenous drug use: The real heterosexual epidemic. *British Journal of Medicine, 294(6569),* 389–90.

Moss, E. (1995). Group supervision: Focus on countertransference. *International Journal of Group Psychotherapy, 45(4),* 537–49.

Mullan, H. (1970). Transference and countertransference: New horizons. In H. Ruitenbeek (Ed.). *Group therapy today* (pp. 216–29). New York: Aronson Press.

Mullan, H., & Rosenbaum, M. (1978). *Group psychotherapy: Theory and practice.* New York: Free Press.

Namir, S., & Sherman, S. (1989). Coping with countertransference. In C. Kain (Ed.). *No longer immune: A counselor's guide to AIDS* (pp. 263–80). Alexandria, Va.: American Association for Counseling and Development.

Navia, B.A., & Price, R.W. (1987). The acquired immunodeficiency syndrome dementia complex as the presenting or sole manifestation of human immodeficiency virus infection. *Archives of Neurology, 44,* 65–69.

Newmark, D.A. (1984). Review of a support group for patients with AIDS. *Topics in Clinical Nursing, 6,* 38–44.

New York State Department of Health AIDS Institute. (1993). Tuberculosis and HIV. *Focus on AIDS, Spring,* 1–3.

Nichols, M. (1989). The forgotten seven percent: Women and AIDS. In C. Kain (Ed.). *No longer immune: A counselor's guide to AIDS* (pp. 77–92). Alexandria, Va.: American Association for Counseling and Development.

Nichols, S.E. (1984). Social and support groups with patients with acquired immune deficiency syndrome. In S.E. Nichols & D.G. Ostrow (Eds.). *Psychiatric implications of acquired immune deficiency syndrome* (pp. 77–82). Washington, D.C.: American Psychiatric Press.

Norsworthy, K., & Horne, A. (1994). Issues in group work with HIV infected gay and bisexual men. *Journal for Specialists in Group Work, 19,* 112–19.

Norton, J. (1963). Treatment of a dying patient. *Psychoanalytic Study of the Child, 18,* 541–60.

Ochberg, F.M. (1991). Post-traumatic therapy. *Psychotherapy, 48(1),* 5–15.

Ochberg, F.M. (1995). *Post-traumatic therapy and victims of violence.* New York: Brunner/Mazel.

Odets, W. (1994). Survivor guilt in seronegative gay men. In S. Cadwell, R. Burham, & M. Forstein (Eds.). *Therapists on the front line: Psychotherapy with gay men in the age of AIDS* (pp. 453–74). Washington, D.C.: American Psychiatric Press.

Oerlemans-Bunn, M. (1988). On being, gay, single and bereaved. *American Journal of Nursing, 4,* 472–77.

Oktay, J. (1992). Burnout in hospital social workers who work with AIDS patients. *Social Work, 37(5),* 432–39.

Ormont, L. (1970). The use of objective countertransference to resolve group resistances. *Group Process, 3,* 95–111.

Ormont, L. (1980). Training group therapists through the study of countertransference. *Group, 17,* 26–33.

Ormont, L. (1988). Leaders' role in resolving resistance to intimacy in the group setting. *International Journal of Group Psychotherapy, 38,* 29–47.

References

Ormont, L. (1990). The craft of bridging. *International Journal of Group Psychotherapy, 40(1)*, 3–30.

Ormont, L. (1992a). Subjective countertransference in the group setting: The modern analytic experience. *International Journal of Group Psychotherapy, 17(1)*, 3–12.

Ormont, L. (1992b). *The group therapy experience: From theory to practice.* New York: St. Martin's Press.

O'Rourke, J., & Sutherland, P. (1994). Negotiating HIV infection in rural America: Breaking through the isolation. In S. Cadwell, R. Burnham, & M. Forstein (Eds.). *Therapists on the front lines: Psychotherapy with gay men in the age of AIDS* (pp. 363–78). Washington, D.C.: American Psychiatric Press.

Palmer, L. (1993). The nurses of Vietnam: Still wounded. *New York Times Magazine, 36*, 42, 48, 52.

Pearlman, L., & Saakvitne, K. (1995a). Treating therapists with vicarious traumatization and secondary traumatic stress disorders. In C. Figley (Ed.). *Compassion fatigue: Coping with secondary traumatic stress disorder in those who treat the traumatized* (pp. 150–77). New York: Brunner/Mazel.

Pearlman, L., & Saakvitne, K. (1995b). *Trauma and the therapist: Countertransference and vicarious traumatization in psychotherapy with incest survivors.* New York: Norton.

Pearlman, R., Cain, K., & Patrick, D. (1993). Insight pertaining to patient assessment of states worse than death. *Journal of Clinical Ethics, 4*, 33–41.

Perry, S., Jacobsberg, L., & Fishman, L. (1989). Suicidal ideation and HIV testing. *Journal of the American Medical Association, 263*, 679–82.

Perry, S., Jacobsberg, L., & Fishman, B. (1990). Relationship between CD4 lymphocytes and psychosocial variables among HIV seropositive adults. *International Conference on AIDS, 6(1)*, 140.

Perry, S., & Jacobsen, P. (1986). Neuropsychiatric manifestations of AIDS-spectrum disorders. *Hospital and Community Psychiatry, 37*, 135–41.

Peterson, J.L., & Marin, G. (1988). Issues in the prevention of AIDS among Black and Hispanic men. *American Psychologist, 43*, 871–77.

Pinderhughes, E. (1983). Empowerment for our clients and for ourselves. *Social Casework, 64(6)*, 331–38.

References

Pines, D. (1986). Working with women survivors of the Holocaust: Affective experiences in transference and countertransference. *International Journal of Psychoanalysis, 67,* 295–307.

Posey, C. (1988). Confidentiality in an AIDS support group. *Journal of Counseling and Development, 66(5),* 226–27.

Quill, T. (1994). Physician-assisted death: Progress or peril? *Suicide and Life Threatening Behaviors, 24,* 315–25.

Rabkin, J., Remien, R.H., Katoff, L.S., & Williams, J.B. (1993). Resilience in adversity among long-term survivors of AIDS. *Hospital and Community Psychiatry, 44,* 162–67.

Rabkin, J., Remien, R., & Wilson, C. (1994). *Good doctors, good patients: Partners in HIV treatment.* New York: NCM.

Rabkin, R., & Rabkin, J. (1994). Management of depression in patients with HIV infection. In W. Odets & M. Shernoff (Eds.). *The second decade of AIDS: A mental health practice handbook* (pp. 11–26). New York: Hatherleigh Press.

Rachlis, A., Peter, A., & Varga, R. (1993). After concorde: Changes in the initiation of zidovudine therapy in Ontario, Canada. *National Conference on Human Retroviruses Related Infections, 1,* 132.

Racker, H. (1953). A contribution to the problem of countertransference. *International Journal of Psychoanalysis, 34,* 313–24.

Racker, H. (1957). The meanings and use of countertransference. *Psychoanalytic Quarterly, 26,* 303–24.

Rando, T.A. (1984). *Grief, dying and death.* Chicago: Research Press.

Rappaport, J. (1985). The power of empowerment of language. *Social Policy, 16(2),* 15–21.

Reamer, F. (1991). AIDS, social work, and the "duty to protect." *Social Work, 36(1),* 56–60.

Remien, R., & Wagner, G. (1994). Counseling long-term survivors of HIV/AIDS. In W. Odets & M. Shernoff (Eds.). *The second decade of AIDS: A mental health practice handbook* (pp. 179–200). New York: Hatherleigh Press.

Renneker, R. (1957). Countertransference reactions to cancer. *Psychosomatic Medicine, 19(5),* 409–19.

Ribble, D. (1989). Psychosocial support groups for people with HIV infection and AIDS. *Holistic Nursing Practice, 3(4),* 52–62.

Riley, L.W. (1993). Drug-resistant tuberculosis. *Clinical Infectious Diseases, 17,* 442–46.

Ringler, K., Whitman, H., Gustafson, J., & Coleman, F. (1981). Tech-

References

nical advances in leading a cancer support group. *International Journal of Psychotherapy, 31(3)*, 329–43.

Roback, H., Ochoa, E., Bloch, F., & Purdon, S. (1992). Guarding confidentiality in clinical groups: The therapist's dilemma. *International Journal of Group Psychotherapy, 42(1)*, 81–103.

Rogers, J., & Britton, P. (1994). AIDS and rational suicide: A counseling psychology perspective or a slide on the slippery slope. *Counseling Psychologist, 22(1)*, 171–78.

Roller, B., & Nelson, V. (1991). *The art of co-therapy: How therapists work together.* New York: Guilford Press.

Rosenberg, P. (1984). Support groups: A special therapeutic entity. *Small Group Behavior, 15*, 173–86.

Rosenthal, L. (1987). *Resolving resistances in group psychotherapy.* New York: Aronson Press.

Rosica, T. (1995). AIDS and boundaries: Instinct versus empathy. *Focus: A Guide to AIDS Research and Counseling, 10(2)*, 1–4.

Rounds, K.A. (1988). AIDS in rural areas: Challenges to providing care. *Journal of Social Work, 33*, 257–61.

Rounds, K.A., Galinsky, M.J., & Stevens, L.S. (1991). Linking people with AIDS in rural communities: The telephone group. *Social Work, 35(1)*, 13–18.

Rozynko, V., & Dondershine, H. (1991). Trauma focus group therapy for Vietnam veterans with PTSD. *Psychotherapy, 28(1)*, 157–61.

Ruskin, C. (1988). *The quilt: Stories from the names project.* New York: Pocket Books.

Sadowy, D. (1991). Is there a role for the psychoanalytic psychotherapist with a patient dying from AIDS? *Psychoanalytic Review, 78(2)*, 199–207.

Sageman, S. (1989). Group therapy for patients with AIDS. In D.A. Halperin (Ed.). *Group psychodynamics: New paradigms and new perspectives* (pp. 125–38). Chicago: Year Book.

Schapiro, F. (1989). Efficacy of the eye movement desensitization procedure in the treatment of traumatic memories. *Journal of Traumatic Stress, 2(2)*, 199–223.

Schapiro, F. (1995). *Eye movement desensitization and reprocessing: Basic principle protocols and procedures.* New York: Guilford Press.

Scheidlinger, S. (1993). History of group psychotherapy. In H. Kaplan & B. Sadock (Eds.). *Comprehensive group psychotherapy* (pp. 2–10). Baltimore: Williams & Wilkins.

References

Schiller, N. (1990). The invisible woman: Caregiving and the construction of AIDS health services. *Culture, Medicine and Psychiatry, 17(4)*, 487–512.

Schneider, S., Taylor, S., Kemeny, M., & Hammen, C. (1991). AIDS related factors predictive of suicidal ideation of low and high intent among gay and bisexual men. *Suicide and Life Threatening Behavior, 21(4)*, 313–28.

Schwartz, W. (1974). The social work in the group. In R. Klenk & R. Ryan (Eds.). *The practice of social work* (pp. 208–28). Belmont, Calif.: Wadsworth Publishing.

Schwartzberg, S. (1992). AIDS-related bereavement among gay men: The inadequacy of current theories of grief. *Psychotherapy, 29(3)*, 422–29.

Searles, H. (1955). The informational value of supervisors' emotional experiences. *Psychiatry, 18*, 135–46.

Seligman, M.E. (1975). *Helplessness: On depression, development and death.* San Francisco: Freeman.

Shay, J.J. (1992). Countertransference in the family therapy of survivors of sexual abuse. *Child Abuse and Neglect, 16*, 585–93.

Shelby, D. (1995). Mourning within a culture of mourning. In S. Cadwell, R. Burnham, & M. Forstein (Eds). *Therapists on the frontline: Psychotherapy with gay men in the age of AIDS* (pp. 53–81). Washington, D.C.: American Psychiatric Press.

Shernoff, M. (1994). Counseling chemically dependent people with HIV illness. In W. Odets & M. Shernoff (Eds.). *The second decade of AIDS: A mental health practice handbook* (pp. 27–46). New York: Hatherleigh Press.

Shilts, R. (1987). *And the band played on.* New York: St. Martin's Press.

Siegel, K. (1986). Psychosocial aspects of rational suicide. *American Journal of Psychotherapy, 40*, 405–18.

Silverman, D. (1993). Psychosocial impact of HIV-related caregiving on health providers: A review and recommendations for the role of psychiatry. *American Journal of Psychiatry, 150(5)*, 705–12.

Simon, S. (1995). Spotlight on ... Gerald Busby, composer. *HIV Art News, Fall/Winter*, 3.

Singer, B. (1983). Psychosocial trauma, defense strategies and treatment considerations in cancer patients and their families. *American Journal of Family Therapy, 11(3)*, 15–21.

Singer, M. (1994). AIDS and the health crisis of the U.S. urban poor:

References

The perspective of critical medical anthropology. *Social Science and Medicine, 39(7)*, 931–46.

Slavson, S. (1950). Transference phenomenon in group psychotherapy. *Psychoanalytic Review, 37*, 39–55.

Slavson, S. (1953). Sources of countertransference and group induced anxiety. *International Journal of Group Psychotherapy, 3*, 373–89.

Smart, T. (1996). Protease inhibitors come of age. *GMHC Treatment Issues 10(2)*, 3–6.

Solomon, A., Loeffler, R., & Frank, G. (1953). An analysis of co-therapist interaction in group psychotherapy. *International Journal of Group Psychotherapy, 3*, 171–80.

Solomon, Z., & Flum, H. (1988). Life events, combat stress reactions and posttraumatic stress disorder. *Social Science Medicine, 26*, 319–26.

Spector, I., & Conklin, R. (1987). Brief reports: AIDS group psychotherapy. *International Journal of Group Psychotherapy, 37(3)*, 433–39.

Spiegel, D., Bloom, J., Kraemer, H., & Gottheil, E. (1989). Effect of psychosocial treatment on survival of patients with metastatic breast cancer. *Lancet, 2(8668)*, 888–91.

Spiegel, D., Bloom, J., & Yalom, I. (1981). Group support for patients with metastatic cancer. *Archives of General Psychiatry, 38(5)*, 527–33.

Spiegel, D., & Glafkides, M. (1983). Effects of group confrontation with death and dying. *International Journal of Group Psychotherapy, 33(4)*, 433–38.

Spotnitz, H. (1968). The management and mastery of resistance in group psychotherapy. *Journal of Group Psychoanalysis 3*, 5–22.

Spotnitz, H. (1987). Transference and countertransference in group. *Modern Psychoanalysis, 12(1)*, 25–34.

Stall, R., Coates, T.J., Mandel, J.S., Morales, E.S., & Sorensen, J.L. (1989). The epidemiology of AIDS: Behavioral factors and intervention. In R.A. Kaslow & D.P. Francis (Eds.) *The epidemiology of HIV/AIDS* (pp. 266–81). New York: Oxford University Press.

Steketee, G., & Foa, E.B. (1989). Rape victims: Posttraumatic stress responses and their treatment; A review of the literature. *Journal of Anxiety Disorders, 1*, 69–88.

Stone, W., Blase, M., & Bozzuto, J. (1980). Late dropouts from group therapy. *American Journal of Psychotherapy, 34*, 401–13.

References

Stone, W., & Rutan, S. (1984). Duration of treatment in group psychotherapy. *International Journal of Group Psychotherapy, 34*, 101–17.

Strawn, J.M. (1987). The psychosocial consequences of AIDS. In J. Durham & F. Cohen (Eds.). *The person with AIDS: Nursing perspectives* (pp. 126–49). New York: Springer.

Stutman, R.K., & Bliss, E.L. (1985). Post-traumatic stress disorder, hypnotizability and imagery. *American Journal of Psychiatry, 142*, 741–43.

Thacker, J.K. (1984). Using psychodrama to reduce burnout in the helping professions. *Journal of Group Psychotherapy, Psychodrama and Sociometry, 40*, 14–25.

Tierney, R. (1990). Newark's serial of drugs and AIDS. *New York Times*, December 16, A1.

Totten, G.T., Lamb, D.H., & Reeder, G.D. (1990). Tarasoff and confidentiality in AIDS related psychotherapy. *Professional Psychology: Research and Practice, 21(3)*, 155–60.

Trice, A. (1988). Posttraumatic stress syndrome-like symptoms among AIDS caregivers. *Psychological Reports, 63*, 656–58.

Tross, S., & Hirsch, D. (1988). Psychological distress and neuropsychological complications of HIV infection and AIDS. *American Psychologist,, 43(11)*, 929–34.

Tunnell, G. (1991). Complications in group psychotherapy with AIDS patients. *International Journal of Group Psychotherapy, 41*, 481–98.

Tunnell, G. (1994). Special issues in group psychotherapy for gay men with AIDS. In S. Cadwell, R. Burnham, & M. Forstein (Eds.). *Therapists on the front lines: Psychotherapy with gay men in the age of AIDS* (pp. 237–54). Washington, D.C.: American Psychiatric Press.

Valente, S. (1994). Psychotherapist reactions to the suicide of a patient. *American Journal of Orthopsychiatric, 64(4)*, 614–21.

van der Kolk, B.A. (1984). *Traumatic stress disorder: Psychological and biological sequelae.* Washington, D.C.: American Psychiatric Press.

van der Kolk, B.A. (1987). The role of the group in the origin and resolution of the trauma response. In B.A. van der Kolk (Ed.). *Psychological trauma* (pp. 153–72). Washington, D.C.: American Psychiatric Press.

Vaughan, J., Wiese, M., Gold, R., & Tarrier, N. (1994). Eye movement desensitization: Symptom change in post-traumatic stress disorder. *British Journal of Psychiatry, 164*, 533–41.

204

References

Volberding, P. (1989). Supporting the health care team in caring for patients with AIDS. *Journal of the American Medical Association, 261(5)*, 747–48.

Wade, K., & Simon, E. (1993). Survival bonding: A response to stress and work with AIDS. *Social Work and Health Care, 19(1)*, 77–89.

Walker, J.I., & Nash, J.L. (1981). Group therapy in the treatment of Vietnam combat veterans. *International Journal of Group Psychotherapy, 31(3)*, 379–89.

Walker, L.E. (1991). Post-traumatic stress disorder in women: Diagnosis and treatment of battered women's syndrome. Special Issue: Psychotherapy with victims. *Psychotherapy, 28*, 21–29.

Ward, M. (1993). A different disease: HIV/AIDS and health care for women in poverty. *Culture, Medicine and Psychiatry, 17*, 413–30.

Weisman, A. (1981). Understanding the cancer patient: The syndrome of care giver's plight. *Psychiatry, 44*, 161–68.

Werth, J. (1992). Rational suicide and AIDS: Considerations for the psychotherapist. *Counseling Psychologist, 20(4)*, 645–59.

Wigren, J.P. (1994). Narrative completion in the treatment of trauma. *Psychotherapy, 31(3)*, 415–23.

Wilson, J.P, Harel, Z., & Kahana, B. (1988). *Human adaptation to extreme stress: From Holocaust to Vietnam.* New York: Plenum.

Wilson, J.P., & Lindy, J. (1995). Theoretical and conceptual foundations of countertransference in post traumatic therapies. In J.P. Wilson & J. Lindy (Ed.). *Countertransference in the treatment of PTSD* (pp. 1–5). New York: Guilford Press.

Wilson, J.P. (1994). The historical evolution of PTSD diagnostic criteria: From Freud to DSM-IV. *Journal of Traumatic Stress, 7(4)*, 681–98.

Winnicott, D.W. (1949). Hate in countertransference. *International Journal of Psychoanalysis, 30*, 60–74.

Wolpe, J., & Abrams, J. (1991). Post traumatic stress disorder overcome by eye-movement desensitization: A case report. *Journal of Behavior Therapy and Experimental Psychiatry, 22*, 39–43.

Yalom, I. (1966). A study of group therapy drop-outs. *Archives of General psychiatry, 14*, 393–414.

Yalom, I. (1970). *The theory and practice of group psychotherapy.* New York: Basic Books.

Yalom, I. (1980). *Existential psychotherapy.* New York: Basic Books.

References

Yalom, I. (1995). *The theory and practice of group psychotherapy.* (4th ed.). New York: Basic Books.

Yalom, I.D., & Greaves, C. (1977). Group therapy with terminally ill. *Journal of Psychiatry, 134(4),* 396–400.

Young, W. (1995). Eye movement desensitization reprocessing: Its use in resolving the trauma caused by the loss of a war buddy. *American Journal of Psychotherapy, 49(2),* 282–91.

Yu, M.M., & O'Neal, B. (1992). Issues of confidentiality when working with persons with AIDS. *Clinical Social Work Journal, 20(4),* 421–30.

Zankowski, G. (1987). Responsive programming: Meeting the needs of chemically dependent women. *Alcoholism Treatment Quarterly, 4(4),* 53–76.

Index